Bubbles, Rainbows, and Worms

Other books by the author:

*Gentle Rain and Loving Sun: Activities for Developing a Healthy
Self-Concept in Young Children*

One, Two, Buckle My Shoe: Math Activities for Young Children

Bubbles, Rainbows, and Worms
Science Experiments for Preschool Children

gryphon house
Beltsville, MD

© 1981, 2004 Sam Ed Brown
Published by Gryphon House, Inc.
10726 Tucker Street, Beltsville, MD 20705
800.638.0928 ○ 301.595.9500 ○ 301.595.0051 (fax)

Visit us on the web at www.gryphonhouse.com

Illustrations: Silas Stamper and Kathi Whelan Dery

Cover photograph: Straight Shots

Library of Congress Cataloging-in-Publication Data

Brown, Sam Ed, 1932-1993
   Bubbles, rainbows, and worms : science experiments for preschool children / by Sam Ed Brown ; illustrations, Kathi Whelan Dery.
      p. cm.
Includes index.
   ISBN 0-87659-241-8
   1. Science--Study and teaching (Preschool) 2. Science--Problems, exercises, etc.--Handbooks, manuals, etc. I. Title.
   LB1140.5.S35B76 2004
   372.3'5--dc22
                                                              2003018173

Table of Contents

The Young Child and Science 7

A Word About Preschool Science
for Teachers 8

Fitting Science Into the
Preschool Classroom 10

10 Commandments for
Science Teachers 11

The Classroom Science Center 12

Materials to Collect 14

Experiences With Air **15**

Blowing Bubbles 16

Which Is Faster? 17

Air, Air, Everywhere 18

Plumber-Plumber 19

Blow the Man Down 20

Wet and Dry 21

Children's Books 22

Experiences With Animals **23**

Animal Baby Puzzles 24

Hunting for Animals 25

Watching Ants 26

Wild Spiders 27

Spider Webs 28

Animal Homes 29

Earthworms 30

From Tadpole to Frog 31

Terrariums 32

Children's Books 33

Experiences With the Environment........**35**

Wind Vanes 36

Silhouettes 37

Making a Compass 38

Making Lightning 39

Static Electricity 40

Charting Temperature 41

Parachute Game 42

Night and Day 43

Learning About the Sun 44

Rotation of the Earth 45

Dressing for the Seasons 46

Seasons 47

Gravity 48

Using a Balance Scale 49

Magnets 50

Growing Crystals 51

Children's Books 53

Experiences With Plants **55**

Seed Party 56

Growing Without Seeds 57

Planting Beans 58

Growing Beans 59

Development 60

Making a Seed Book 61

Children's Garden 62

Seeds and Fruits 63

Children's Books 64

Experiences With the Senses...............**65**

Washing and Feeling 66

Sounds Around Us 67

Music Everywhere 68

Hello, Who's There? 69

Tasting 70

What Is That Smell? 71

Exploring Odors 72

Touching 73

Children's Books 74

Experiences With Water 75

Making Steam 76

Making Clouds 77

Water and Ice 78

Water Trick 79

Floating Objects 80

Experimenting With Water 81

Evaporation 82

Making Frost 83

Fish Breathe 84

Children's Books 85

Miscellaneous Experiences 87

Learning About Transportation 88

Transportation 89

Roll on Big Wheels 90

Creating Colors 91

Collections 92

Food Book 93

Children's Books 94

Teacher Resource Books 95

Index 97

Book Index 103

The Young Child and Science

"Why did that happen?" "Why does it work that way?" "What can I do to change that?" "And what will happen if...?"

Young children ask these questions daily. Adults teach young children to teach themselves about science. Preschool science is about process rather than product. With adults and older children, teaching may be verbal. But not with young children. To truly understand the definition of a word, children must act physically on a concept in which the word was used. When children have tested a concept by exploration and manipulation, then it has meaning.

Children do not have to be taught to explore, question, and manipulate; they are born with a powerful desire to do all. Their need to handle, manipulate, and explore has been called many things by psychologists and educators who suggest that this drive sets the stage for future learning. Children derive satisfaction from manipulating and controlling materials and experiences outside their bodies. This drive leads to clarification and understanding.

When children explore the physical world, they add new knowledge to their accumulated store. That newly acquired knowledge becomes the foundation for developing new concepts.

By handling, manipulating, tasting, and feeling, children are able to integrate this information into pre-existing concepts. Thus, children expand and deepen their understanding about the world around them. They broaden their concepts of weight and mass as they float objects in a container of water. They better understand air pressure and movement when they drop feathers and watch them float to the ground. They gain insight concerning life processes as they care for animals and plants.

Science is taught in preschool not to train future scientists and engineers (although we may be doing this), but rather, to equip the child with basic survival skills in this modern, complex world.

In this age of dwindling resources, we must emphasize conservation rather than disposal. If we are to teach conservation, we must help children understand scientific principles. It is only through understanding the physical properties of air, water, soil, weather, and other natural phenomena that future leaders can solve the ever-mounting problems facing the world.

A Word About Preschool Science for Teachers

At present, teachers in kindergarten and childcare, as well as parents of young children, feel presure to do well in literacy and math. Science is often approached on a haphazard basis rather than a time of fun and discovery for both adult and child.

MATERIALS FOR TEACHING

Teaching materials for preschool science are easily acquired. They are all around. Common, ordinary materials are abundant. For example, the container of milk served at lunch. Where does the milk come from? This question may lead to a unit on cows, farm animals, animal babies, animal products, or domestication of animals. All this from one question! And this does not even consider the question of how the milk gets to the school, what happens to it before it arrives, how it is made safe to drink, what is added to it, or who buys it. Not to mention why it has to be made safe, why we drink it, which other animals give milk, that humans are mammals, what mammals are, and why mammals give milk. And still we haven't looked at nutrition, the container itself, the print on the container, storage of milk and many, many other concepts.

Young children do not learn from things that do not interest them; they simply brush them aside. They are interested in materials and objects that attract them and capture their attention. Young children carry things in their pockets that are of no value to anyone else: a colored rock, a marble, sea glass, bent nails, pieces of plants, and perhaps (wonder of wonders) a snake skin or mashed, dried frog. Teachers should be quick to capitalize on the natural curiosity of young children by providing a discovery or science table where a child may bring treasures to show off to the class (properly labeled with his or her name) and show interest in their discoveries. It is a joy to watch a child hard at work looking through seed catalogs and books containing pictures of common plants of the region, trying to find the picture of a plant brought in.

No "special" equipment or supplies are needed for an effective science program. Let the children supply the majority of the materials needed for the program. At times it will be necessary to ask the children to bring in special things for an activity. However, these items are seldom expensive and most parents are eager to supply things such as salt, flour, ammonia, nails, and tacks.

USE REAL OBJECTS, FAMILIAR TO THE CHILD, FOR TEACHING

Preschool science is about the use of real, concrete objects. A child needs to have the object in hand or in sight so that he or she can actively feel and see the properties of the object.

The problem with using elaborate "do not touch" materials for a classroom demonstration is that children will learn little from the materials because they do not know them. This is why we use common, everyday objects. If a teacher wants to introduce new materials to preschool children, the new materials must be left out for children to explore before they are used.

MATERIALS MUST RELATE TO THE REAL WORLD

One preschool teacher did an elaborate display of a beautifully designed model of the solar system, complete with sun, planets, and moons that revolved around the planets. The object was to explain to the children where "shooting stars" come from and why we can see them. Not only had the teacher worked with objects the children knew nothing about (even though she did identify them verbally), but the teacher talked about things that were not a real part of the child's world. The real world in this case is that world with which the child has sustained day-to-day contact. To be successful, preschool teachers must be able to project themselves into the world of the child and see things as the child sees them. Children can identify heat, light, growth, the sun, and night and day. After the child knows what the sun is and does, then the teacher can explain rotation of the planets. Teachers sometimes forget that everything is new and wonderful to a young child.

CHILDREN MUST BE PRESENTED WITH AN ORDERLY SEQUENCE OF FACTS

Programs that are most successful with young children, such as the one developed by Maria Montessori, seek to develop a curriculum that is both orderly and sequential. While adults are more successful in dealing with unrelated facts, they still have difficulties. Programmed learning kits have proved to be highly successful with adults. Both adults and young children learn best with an orderly, sequenced curriculum.

Fitting Science into a Preschool Classroom

Preschool science does not always have to be taught as a separate subject. Science can be a part of many kinds of learning. Consider, for example, language development. A language development lesson directed toward verbal descriptions of shapes and likenesses and differences offers an excellent opportunity for a lesson on fruits and seeds. Fruits such as apples, oranges, bananas, peaches, and others can be examined, tasted, felt, smelled, and described by the children. Facts, such as which fruits have seeds that may be eaten (bananas) and which do not, and which fruits have skins that may be eaten (peaches, apples), and which ones do not can be discussed. Other subjects such as differences in color, texture, shape, the place where each fruit is grown, may also be discussed and described.

Another example falls in the area of fine-motor development, Rather than having children work on commercial puzzles, the teacher can construct a puzzle by dividing a carrot into several pieces. Parsnips or turnips might also be used. Allowing children to work with puzzles like this will help them to understand how parts make a whole.

TEACHING CHILDREN

How do we teach children? To be honest, we do not really teach children, we provide an environment that encourages and allows children to teach themselves. This environment must be rich and sustaining to promote growth and learning.

Modeling is a powerful teaching tool. Learning takes place as the young child observes the attitudes, habits, and actions of the teacher performing a task such as taking care of plants in the classroom. The young child sees the teacher's attitude toward plants, observing how the teacher cares for the plants, not how they are told to care for them. Teachers often create an atmosphere for learning through modeling.

Teachers must provide the needed emotional support and love that will allow children to value themselves as worthy and successful. Children must be rewarded for success and for appropriate behavior if they are to learn that there is justification for their behavior and positive value for learning.

10 Commandments for Teaching Science to Children

1. Give every child a chance to be a part of the experience with special emphasis on the use of the senses.

2. Make activities non-threatening.

3. Be patient with children.

4. Allow the children to control the time you spend on an activity.

5. Always use open-ended questions.

6. Give children ample time to answer questions.

7. Don't expect "standard" reactions and "standard" actions from children.

8. Always accept divergent answers.

9. Encourage observation.

10. Always look for ways to extend the activity.

The Classroom Science Center

A science center is an integral part of any preschool classroom. The amount of equipment a teacher can afford for the center is not nearly as important as the interest and enthusiasm generated by the children. It is very important that the children know that the teacher is interested in the things they are interested in and wonder about, and feel encouraged to bring things to the classroom to share with the class. After the children are sure that it is all right to bring things in, the classroom will soon have a collection of beautiful, wonderful items. Items that interest children may range from rock collections to mashed bottle caps.

SETTING UP THE CENTER

Most teachers have access to some equipment and supplies, so the following large items are suggested:

> table with two or three chairs
> bookcase
> shelves for storage and display
> large metal or plastic tub
> rugs on the floor
> large stool
> magnifier

SMALL EQUIPMENT

As discussed earlier, the children can furnish most supplies needed for preschool science. However, a few necessary items should be on hand:

- different size coils of rope
- measuring devices
- magnifying glasses
- balance and spring scales
- small and large mirrors

LOCATION OF THE CENTER

The location of the science center often depends on the space available. Certain factors should be taken into consideration, such as the ebb and flow of children in the room. If possible, the science center should be located out of the general traffic flow and in a clearly defined space. One method is to block off the area using toy or book shelves.

The science center is a "touch and do center," not a display area. It is possible to find beautifully arranged, well-equipped centers designated for visitors only. In some schools, display items even leave outlines of dust when lifted.

First, and most importantly, the center must attract children. It must be a place where they want to work. If children are not eager to be in the science center it is probably because it is not interesting to them, not because they are not interested in science.

Children are eager to learn. They especially love the science center if it offers interesting things to see, do, smell, taste, and feel. Any teacher can have a successful center and succeed in teaching science if allowed to think like a child and permit her or himself to wonder and not be afraid to learn with the children.

The activities in this book are designed specifically for preschool children. The selected activities are designed to stimulate teachers to begin with the basic experiences and go from there. Each activity presented may be extended indefinitely.

USE OF VOCABULARY

Included with each of the experiments in this book is a section called "Words to Discuss" which gives suggested vocabulary to introduce to children. Young children are very verbal; they bring a wealth of words to any particular activity. However, a young child may be unsure of words in his or her vocabulary. Through experimentation and usage, children learn to define and refine the use of previously undefined words. It is very important that children learn the vocabulary associated with a particular concept.

For these reasons, a teacher should not limit vocabulary when speaking of a concept because the words used are too hard for the child. Some words that are difficult for the children must be used because they are the only words that apply. For example, when exploring the concept of gravity, one cannot expect the child to understand what causes gravity. The child can, however, learn how gravity affects objects that are dropped. "Gravity" can become a part of the vocabulary of the young child, even though the child cannot explain the concept.

Teachers must strive for language enrichment by means of a wide use of different words.

GOOD LUCK!

Materials to Collect

liquid detergent

powdered detergent

straws

crayons

paper cups

construction paper

tempera paint

chair

plastic bottle

rubber bands

paper bags

plastic zipper-closure bags

rubber gloves

paper of various kinds
and sizes

sink plungers

balloons

cans with lids removed

rock salt

books

paper towels

glasses (glass and plastic)

scissors

glue

thumbtacks

cotton

digging tools

cake pans

plaster of Paris

yarn

gravel

balls

heavy and light string

different textures of cloth

corks

plastic tubing

rubber tubing

aquarium

cage

green, leafy vegetables

sand

small plants

sticks

sponges

charcoal

potting soil

rocks

springs

salt

adhesive spray

talcum powder

screen wire

fishing weights

pencils

pins

assorted magnets

feather

needle

comb

thermometer

flashlight

magnifying glass

globe

scale (small)

produce or meat trays

Epsom salt

microscopes

books about animals

books about plants

egg cartons

hot plate

markers

food coloring

prism

milk cartons

assorted wheels

assorted nails

lamp

Experiences With Air

Blowing Bubbles

Which Is Faster?

Air, Air, Everywhere

Plumber-Plumber

Blow the Man Down

Wet and Dry

Children's Books

Blowing Bubbles

PRINCIPLES

Air is a real substance with weight. Light shows all the colors of the rainbow when it passes through a bubble.

MATERIALS

liquid detergent
water
cups
straws
construction paper
crayons

WORDS TO DISCUSS

blow
bubbles
circle
colors
liquid
pop
reflect

SCIENCE EXPERIENCE

○ Put a small amount of soap and water in cups so each child has a cup of soapy water.

○ Dip the end of a straw into the cup, remove the straw, and allow the soapy mixture to drip once. Blow gently and produce a bubble.

○ Talk about the air inside the bubble and point out that the bubble has different colors because light changes when it shines through the bubble.

○ Ask the children why they think bubbles burst when they hit the ground.

○ When it is time to finish the activity, allow the children to catch some of the bubbles on construction paper. Discuss why the popped bubble leaves a wet circle.

○ Allow the children to draw around the wet outline to make designs.

EXPLANATION

Light contains all the colors of the rainbow. When light passes through the bubble, it reflects and is broken into wavelengths, allowing the different colors to be seen. Wet rings on the construction paper show that a bubble is composed of bubble solution surrounding air.

16

Which Is Faster?

PRINCIPLES

Air is all around us. Air affects the way things move.

SCIENCE EXPERIENCE

- Crumple one piece of paper in a ball. Talk about how wadded paper and smooth paper are alike and different.
- Ask the children if they think both weigh the same. Let a child weigh them on a simple balance scale.
- Ask the children if they think the two pieces of paper will fall at the same speed if you dropped them together. Climb on a chair, hold one piece in each hand and drop them. "Why does the crumpled paper fall faster?"

MATERIALS

two pieces of paper
chair

WORDS TO DISCUSS

air
crumpled
flat
pressure
surface

EXPLANATION

As the flat piece of paper falls, it has to push through the air with a larger surface. Since there is more air putting pressure on the flat piece of paper, it falls more slowly. Children sometimes think that the larger or heavier an object is, the faster it will fall. The reason some things fall faster than others depends on the amount of friction or drag from the air.

17

Air, Air, Everywhere

PRINCIPLES

Air is real. Air has substance.

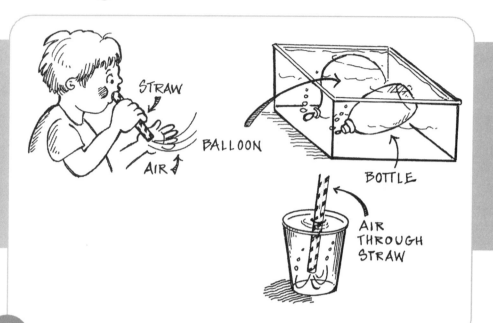

MATERIALS

empty plastic bottle
container
water
balloons
straws
paper bags

WORDS TO DISCUSS

air transfer
blow
bubbles

SCIENCE EXPERIENCE

- Put an empty plastic bottle into a container of water and watch the bubbles come to the surface.
- Blow up a balloon and hold it shut. Place the mouth of the balloon under the water, and then release air from the balloon.
- Allow the children to feel the air coming from a straw when they blow through it. Allow the children to blow through the straw into the water.
- Give the children paper bags. Invite them to blow air into the bags and explore how the air fills the bags.

EXPLANATION

Air bubbles float up to the surface from the straw and the balloon because air is lighter than water.

18

Plumber-Plumber

PRINCIPLES

Air is real. Air has body and weight. Air leaving a space can create a vacuum.

SCIENCE EXPERIENCE

○ Allow the children to explore a plunger. Talk about its use.
○ Push two plumber's friends against each other until they stick.
○ Let the children handle the plungers. "Why are they stuck together?" "What happened to the air when they were pushed together?"

MATERIALS

two plungers (plumber's friends)

WORDS TO DISCUSS

air pressure
plunger
pull
push
stuck
suction
vacuum

EXPLANATION

When a plunger head is pushed against a flat surface, the air is forced out, creating a vacuum. The pressure of the air on the outside of the plunger head is so strong that the head will stay stuck until air seeps in. If two plungers are pushed against each other, a larger and stronger vacuum is created, and the air pressure from both sides holds them together.

19

Blow the Man Down

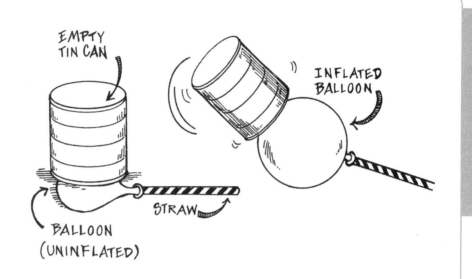

EMPTY TIN CAN

INFLATED BALLOON

STRAW

BALLOON (UNINFLATED)

MATERIALS

tin can
balloons
straws
rubber bands
paperback book
paper lunch bag

WORDS TO DISCUSS

air
blow
pressure
tip
top
straw

SCIENCE EXPERIENCE

- Stand an empty tin can on a table and ask the children try to blow it over (to see how difficult it is). Tell the children you can show them how to blow it over.
- Attach a balloon to the end of a straw with a rubber band.
- Place the can on top of the balloon. Blow through the straw and the balloon will fill, tipping the can.
- Stand a book on end and ask the children to try to blow it over.
- Place the book on a paper lunch bag. Blow into the bag, tipping over the book.
- Let the children try.

EXPLANATION

Air pushes on objects and moves them. This is called air pressure. The air in the balloon can move objects, while blowing on the object cannot, because air in the balloon cannot escape in another direction. Air that children blow can stream around an object, putting less pressure on it.

20

Wet and Dry

Air takes up space. Air has substance.

SCIENCE EXPERIENCE

- Tell the children you are going to put a paper towel under the water without getting the towel wet.
- Crumple up a paper towel and put it in the bottom of the cup.
- Push the glass completely underneath the water, open end first. Make sure the glass is not tilted. When the glass is lifted out of the water, the paper will be dry.
- Again, push the glass with the paper in it beneath the water. This time, allow the cup to tilt. Let the children see the air escape, and watch the water replace the air. This time, the paper will be wet.
- Put the materials in the sand and water table and encourage the children to experiment with the materials.

MATERIALS

paper towels
clear plastic drinking
   cup
pan of water

WORDS TO DISCUSS

air
air pressure
compression
dry
paper
replacement
tilt
wet

EXPLANATION

When a glass is forced straight down into the water, the air inside the glass cannot escape and is compressed in the glass. The compressed air will not allow the water to reach the paper. When the glass is tilted, the air escapes and is replaced by the water.

21

Air

Children's Books

Air—Our Environment by McDougall, Littell, & Co.

Air Is All Around You by Franklyn M. Branley

Airplanes and Flying Machines by Pascale de Bourgoing

The Amazing Air Balloon by Jean Van Leeuwen

Bubble, Bubble by Mercer Mayer

Bubbly Bubble by Colleen A. Hitchcock

Can You See the Wind? by Allan Fowler

Curious George and the Hot Air Balloon by H.A. Rey

Feel the Wind by Arthur Dorros

Gilberto and the Wind by Marie Hall Ets

The Great Balloon Race by Rosie Heywood

Hot-Air Henry by Mary Calhoun

I Like Weather by Aileen Fisher

I Wonder Why Soap Makes Bubbles: And Other Questions About Science by Barbara Taylor

Let's Try It Out in the Air: Hands-On Early-Learning Science Activities by Seymour Simon

Millicent and the Wind by Robert Munsch

The Science Book of Air by Neil Ardley and Nicole Fauteux

Pop! A Book About Bubbles by Kimberly Brubaker Bradley

Science in the Air (How and Why Science) by World Book

Science With Air by Usborne Books

Weather Words and What They Mean by Gail Gibbons

When the Wind Stops by Charlotte Zolotow

The Wind Blew by Pat Hutchins

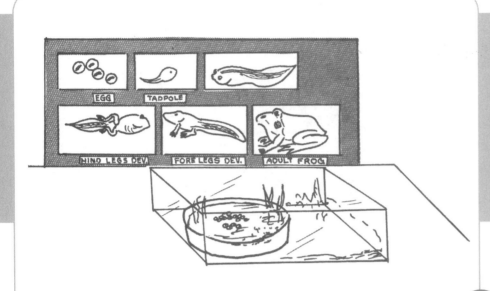

EGG TADPOLE HIND LEGS DEV. FORE LEGS DEV. ADULT FROG

2

Experiences With
Animals

Animal Baby Puzzles

Hunting for Animals

Watching Ants

Wild Spiders

Spider Webs

Animal Homes

Earthworms

From Tadpole to Frog

Terrariums

Children's Books

Animal Baby Puzzles

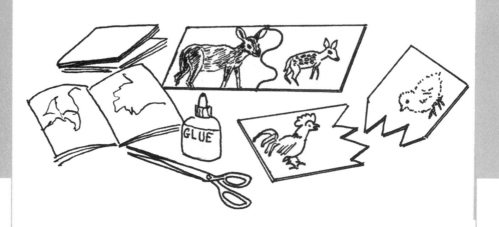

MATERIALS

magazines
old story books
scissors
glue
strips of posterboard or
    heavy paper

WORDS TO DISCUSS

adults
animals
babies
growing
matching

SCIENCE EXPERIENCE

- Spend time with the children finding and cutting out pictures of animals and babies.
- Select pictures of animals and pictures of each animal with its baby.
- Glue the picture of the adult animal on one end of a strip of posterboard and the picture of the baby animal on the other end of the strip.
- Cut the strips in half in different ways to produce puzzles. Mix several strips together and ask the children to match the correct animal with the correct baby.

EXPLANATION

Baby animals look like their parents because they are younger versions of the parent. When a baby animal grows up, it will look just like its parent.

24

Hunting for Animals

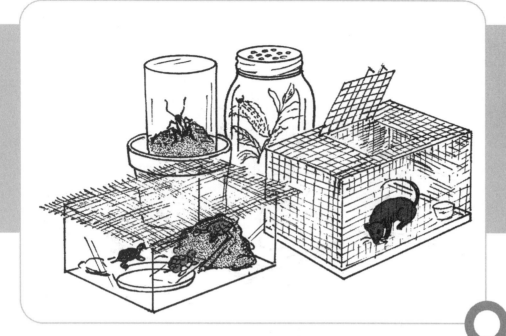

SCIENCE EXPERIENCE

○ From time to time, children bring insects from outside into the classroom, or they bring their pets to school.

○ You may also provide pets and a place where children can care for pets or study insects.

○ Ask the children questions. "Where does the animal or insect live?" "What does the animal or insect eat?" "What does it do?" "What special care is needed?"

○ Develop different units, depending on whether the children have brought in insects or animals.

NOTE: Insects should be kept for only a short time before being released. Model correct behavior toward insects and animals, and mention that wild animals and insects live happier and healthier lives than animals in captivity.

MATERIALS

aquarium with a screen on top
small cage or other suitable container for animals and/or insects

WORDS TO DISCUSS

captivity
care
environment
nature
pet
wild

EXPLANATION

Children need to learn while they are very young to value animal and plant life. Animals and insects need special care when kept by humans because they are in an environment that is not natural to them. They cannot find their own food and water, so people must provide sustenance for them.

25

Watching Ants

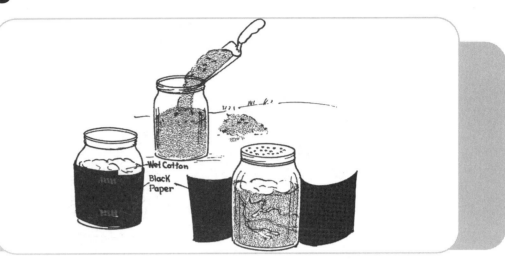

SCIENCE EXPERIENCE

- Fill a clear unbreakable jar half full of dirt.
- Take your children on a science walk to find an anthill. Observe ants coming and going to the hill carrying food.
- Talk about the ant hill and how a family of ants lives together in the hill, and then dig up the ant hill, including the surrounding dirt and debris, and place all in the jar.
- Place dark paper over the top of the jar to encourage the ants to go underground. A piece of cotton that is kept damp on the dirt will supply the ants with the moisture they need.
- Discuss how ants live in colonies, what ants eat, how ants store and care for their eggs, and each ant's specific job.
- The ants may be fed once or twice weekly by adding crumbs of cookies or bread to the jar. Occasionally, add a spoon of honey to the jar.

NOTE: When a clean unbreakable jar is used, children can observe tunnels that are close to the sides. Like other insects, ants should only be kept for a short period of time in an artificial environment. Ants should not be kept longer than a month.

MATERIALS

one-gallon clear
 unbreakable jar
anthill (found outside)
digging tool
dark paper
cotton

WORDS TO DISCUSS

anthill
colony
tunnel
worker ant
queen ant

EXPLANATION

Ants are very social and live together in colonies. Some ants dig tunnels to create a home to care for the eggs laid by the queen. Every ant has its own job: digging, finding food, defending and cleaning the nest, or caring for eggs.

26

Wild Spiders

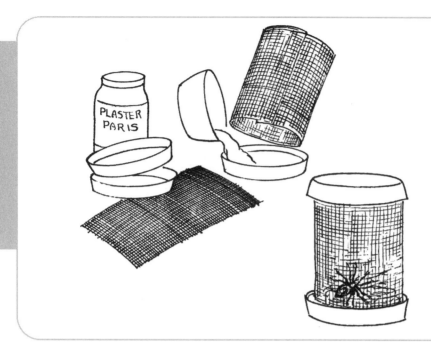

SCIENCE EXPERIENCE

○ Build a cage for a spider, butterfly, ladybug, or beetle by putting a small amount of plaster of Paris into a cake/pie pan and placing the wire cylinder on its end in the plaster of Paris.

○ After it is dry, place a wet sponge, a few sticks, and a spider or other insect in the cylinder. Cover the top with a cake/pie pan.

○ Occasionally add insects for the spider to eat.

MATERIALS

plaster of Paris
two disposable cake/
    pie pans
wire cylinder (rolled up
    wire or screen-tied)
sponge
sticks
spider

WORDS TO DISCUSS

captivity
habitat
insect homes
plaster of Paris
reproduction
spider
sponge

EXPLANATION

If an animal is given everything it needs to survive, it can live in captivity. Animals in captivity must have living spaces that are similar to their natural habitats.

27

Spider Webs

Spiders make their webs from substances in their own bodies. Different spiders make different webs. Spiders use sticky webs to catch food.

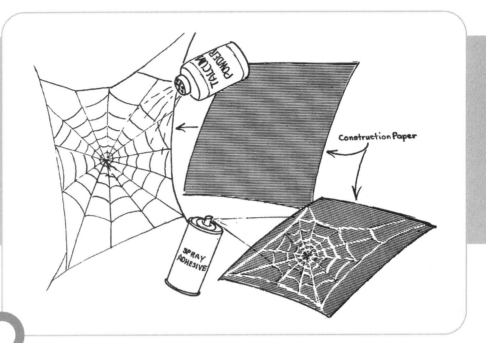

Construction Paper

MATERIALS

black construction paper
talcum powder
spray adhesive

WORDS TO DISCUSS

capture
eat
insect
sticky
web

SCIENCE EXPERIENCE

○ Take the children on a walk to hunt for spider webs.
○ Locate a spider web in the building or outside on the bushes.
○ Help the children sprinkle talcum powder on the web and carefully lift it up with the paper until it is free and secured on the paper. Spray with spray adhesive.
○ Look for webs that are different. Discuss how spiders spin webs to catch insects, how spiders eat these insects, and how the web is sticky so the insects will stick to the web. The library will have books with pictures of spiders and webs.

EXPLANATION

Spiders secrete sticky material from their bodies to build their webs. Different spiders build different types of webs to trap bugs for food. Webs are very strong and can stretch without breaking, so spiders can catch large bugs. Spiders don't get caught in the webs because the little tips of their legs have special oil on them.

28

Animal Homes

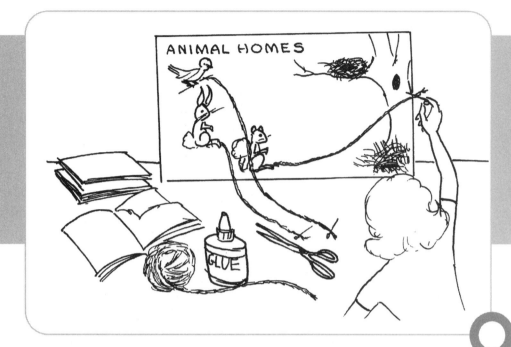

Animals have homes. Different kinds of animals have different kinds of homes.

SCIENCE EXPERIENCE

- Let the children cut pictures from magazines of animals and homes where animals live.
- Divide a posterboard in half. On one half, glue pictures of animals. On the other half, glue pictures of animal homes.
- Cut yarn into two-foot lengths. Use a hole punch to punch a hole beside each picture. Attach one end of the string to a picture of an animal.
- Encourage children to find the home that belongs to that animal and to attach the other end of the string to the correct hole.

MATERIALS

pictures of animals
pictures of animal homes
posterboard
yarn
glue

WORDS TO DISCUSS

burrow
cave
hill
jungle
nest
predators

EXPLANATION

All animals need shelter sometimes. They build their homes in the safest places they can find, to protect themselves and their babies from predators and harsh weather.

29

Earthworms

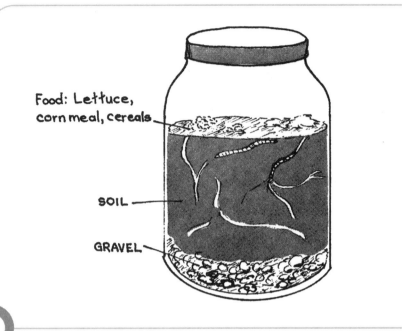

Food: Lettuce, cornmeal, cereals

SOIL

GRAVEL

PRINCIPLES

Living things need different environments for survival.

MATERIALS

large (one- to two-gallon, three- to six-liter) large–mouth glass jar
soil
earthworms
gravel
food for worms (lettuce, cornmeal, cereals)

WORDS TO DISCUSS

adapt
burrow
food
gravel
observe
soil
underground

SCIENCE EXPERIENCE

○ Mix a small amount of gravel in rich planting soil. Put earthworms in the jar. Add food such as lettuce, cornmeal, and cereal on top of the soil and keep the soil moist but not wet.
○ Children can observe the earthworms in a natural environment.
○ Discuss the way the worms burrow and live underground, and how they adapt to their new environment.

EXPLANATION

Earthworms live underground because they must stay moist to survive. They burrow in the ground, eating and moving dirt around. If a worm is too hot, too cold, or too wet, it will look for a better place to burrow. That's why we see worms on the sidewalk when it is raining.

From Tadpole to Frog

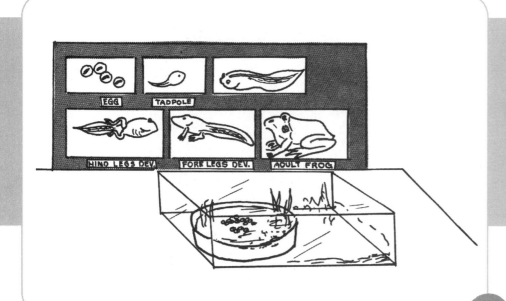

PRINCIPLES

Not all baby animals look like their parents. Animals in cages need special care.

SCIENCE EXPERIENCE

- Put frog eggs, pond water, and plants in the container. Watch daily for frog eggs to hatch. Rocks should be supplied so the tadpoles can climb up for air as they grow. If you use a gallon jug for egg hatching, it is best to change containers as the tadpoles develop.
- After the eggs begin to hatch, provide green vegetables for food for the tadpoles.
- Let the children observe that tadpoles do not look like frogs. Encourage them to continue to watch as the hind legs and front legs begin to grow and the tail grows smaller.
- Discuss the changes taking place, hatching of the eggs, what frogs and tadpoles eat, and how frogs and tadpoles breathe.

MATERIALS

frog eggs
pond water and plants
green leafy vegetables
water tank or water
    container (a one-gallon
    or three-liter jug
    will do)

WORDS TO DISCUSS

amphibian
hatch
gills
tadpole

EXPLANATION

Frogs are animals that live in the water like fish when they are babies, but when they grow into adults they live on the land. Animals that grow this way are called amphibians. When they are babies, they are called tadpoles, and they breathe underwater through gills on their sides. As they grow, they lose their gills and tails and grow legs so they can live out of the water.

31

Terrariums

Plants can use the same air and water over and over again. People can build homes for plants.

MATERIALS

one large one- or two-gallon (three- to six-liter) plastic jar for the whole class or a quart size (one-liter) plastic jar for each child
gravel
soil
sand
small plants
small lid to hold water

WORDS TO DISCUSS

air
carbon dioxide
oxygen
plants
sand
soil
terrarium
water

SCIENCE EXPERIENCE

- The class can create one large terrarium or individual terrariums.
- Instruct the children to cover the bottom half of their jars with gravel. Next, ask them to mix soil and sand together, one part sand and four parts soil, and place a layer of the soil mixture on the gravel.
- Small plants such as ferns and moss may be planted in this soil.
- Put water in a small lid and place it in the jar so the plants have water.
- Add decorations such as colored gravel or miniature animals. Screw the lid on tightly and the terrarium is complete.
- Talk about how the plants reuse the same air and water.

EXPLANATION

A simple explanation is enough for children. They will understand more about plants as they see that neither air nor water needs to be added to the plants' environment. Talk about the way animals breathe in oxygen and breathe out carbon dioxide. Tell the children that plants breathe carbon dioxide and give off oxygen. This means that plants and animals help each other to breathe.

32

Animals

1, 2, 3 to the Zoo by Eric Carle

An Extraordinary Egg by Leo Lionni

Animal Babies by Holly Ann Shelowitz

Animal Colors by Brian Wildsmith

Animals in Winter by Henrietta Bancroft

Beetles and Bugs by Audrey Wood

Birds by Brian Wildsmith

Crictor by Tomi Ungerer

Early Morning in the Barn by Nancy Tafuri

Earthworms by Chris Henwood

Felix and the 400 Frogs by Jon Buller and Susan Schade

The *Frederick* books by Leo Lionni

Frog on His Own by Mercer Mayer

Frogs and Toads and Tadpoles, Too by Allan Fowler

From Tadpole to Frog by Wendy Pfeffer

Growing Frogs by Vivian French

Hungry Animals: My First Look at a Food Chain by Pamela Hickman

Jump, Frog, Jump! by Robert Kalan

Let's Go Home, Little Bear by Martin Waddell and Barbara Firth

The Life and Times of the Ant by Charles Micucci

Little Polar Bear by Hans de Beer

The Magic School Bus on the Ocean Floor by Joanna Cole

Miss Spider's Tea Party by David Kirk

A New Butterfly: My First Look at Metamorphosis by Pamela Hickman

The Ocean Alphabet Book by Jerry Palotta

One Hundred Hungry Ants by Elinor J Pinczes

Owl at Home by Arnold Lobel

Children's Books

Owl Babies by Martin Waddell

Owl Moon by Jane Yolen

Python's Party by Brian Wildsmith

Rooster's Off to See the World by Eric Carle

SPLASH! by Ann Jonas

Starfish by Edith Thacher Hurd

Thanks to Cows by Allan Fowler

There's an Alligator Under my Bed by Mercer Mayer

The Very Hungry Caterpillar by Eric Carle

What's Alive? by Kathleen Weidner Zoehfeld

What Do You Do With a Tail Like This? by Steve Jenkins

What Lives in a Shell? by Kathleen Weidner Zoehfeld

Who Lives Here? by Dorothea Deprisco

Wiggly Worms by Ladybird Books

Wild Moms! by Ginjer L. Clarke

The Wind Blew by Pat Hutchins

Windy Day by Janet Palazzo

Experiences With the
Environment

Wind Vanes
Silhouettes
Making a Compass
Making Lightning
Static Electricity
Charting Temperature
Parachute Game
Night and Day
Learning About the Sun
Rotation of the Earth
Dressing for the Seasons
Seasons
Gravity
Using a Balance Scale
Magnets
Growing Crystals
Children's Books

Wind Vanes

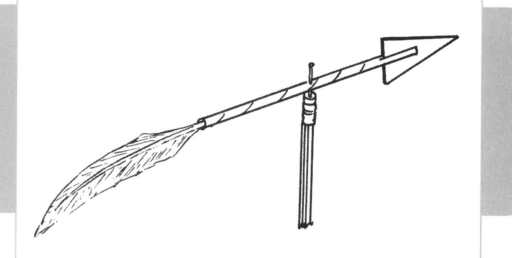

PRINCIPLES

The wind blows from different directions. We can record which way it blows.

MATERIALS

drinking straw
feather
arrowhead (cut arrowhead
    with a long shank from
    cardboard)
straight pin
pencil with eraser
long stick

WORDS TO DISCUSS

direction (North, South,
    East, West)
light wind
strong wind
vane
wind

SCIENCE EXPERIENCE

○ Put a feather in one end of a straw and put a cardboard arrowhead in the other end (fold the shank of the arrowhead and push it into the straw).

○ Put the pin through the middle of the straw with the point going into the eraser of the pencil, so the straw can spin freely on the pin. Tie the pencil to a long stick.

○ Children may take their wind vanes outside to see how the wind moves them.

○ Help the children keep a daily record of which way the wind is blowing. "Is there a relationship between the way the wind is blowing and the weather?" "How many days this week was the wind blowing?" "Was it a strong wind?"

EXPLANATION

It can be difficult for young children to understand how a wind vane works. Demonstrate by blowing on the feather that the air (wind) forces the wind vane to turn until the wind no longer hits it from the side. When the wind vane has finished turning, the arrow will be pointing toward you. Tell the children that wind blows because the air around the earth is always moving.

36

Silhouettes

PRINCIPLES

Objects that block light cause shadows.

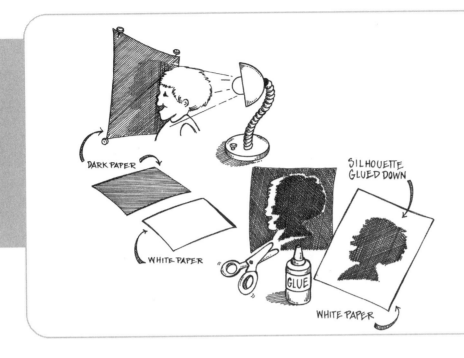

DARK PAPER

WHITE PAPER

SILHOUETTE GLUED DOWN

GLUE

WHITE PAPER

SCIENCE EXPERIENCE

- Use thumbtacks or tape to attach a sheet of paper to the wall. Place a lamp on the table in front of the paper.
- Place a chair sideways between the lamp and the paper and ask the child to sit in the chair facing forward.
- Trace the outlines of the child's shadow on the paper. Explain to the children that their shadows are called silhouettes.
- Allow the child to cut out and mount the silhouette on dark-colored construction paper. "What made the shadow?" Ask the children if they think the silhouette looks like them. "Where is your nose in your silhouette?" "Does your nose in the silhouette look like your nose when you look in the mirror?"

MATERIALS

thumbtacks or masking tape
large sheets of butcher paper
scissors
glue
dark construction paper

WORDS TO DISCUSS

shadow
silhouette

EXPLANATION

The children can see shadows on the wall because objects between the lamp and the wall keep the light from hitting the wall.

37

Making a Compass

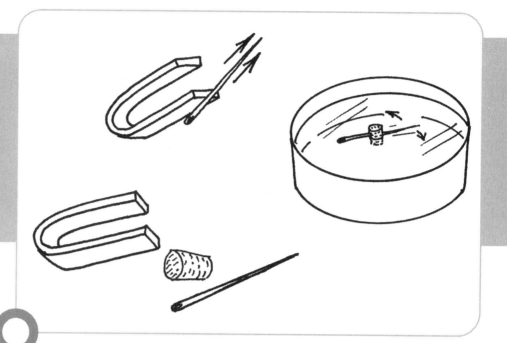

PRINCIPLES

Magnets attract certain objects. A compass can determine which direction a person is going (North, South, East, or West).

MATERIALS

cork
needle
pan of water
magnet
compass

WORDS TO DISCUSS

attract
compass
magnet
magnetize

SCIENCE EXPERIENCE

○ Stroke a pin 30 to 50 times with a magnet, always in the same direction, to magnetize the pin.

○ Stick the pin through a cork and float the cork in the water. "Which way does the pin float?" "If you lift it out of the water and put it back, will it point the same way?"

○ Talk about the North Pole and the fact that compass points are attracted to the North. Discuss how knowing this can help a person who is lost.

CAUTION: Supervise closely.

○ Let the children explore using a compass.

EXPLANATION

Certain parts of magnets are always attracted to certain parts of other magnets. Compass needle points are attracted to the North because the Earth acts as a giant magnet and compass points are small magnets.

38

Making Lightning

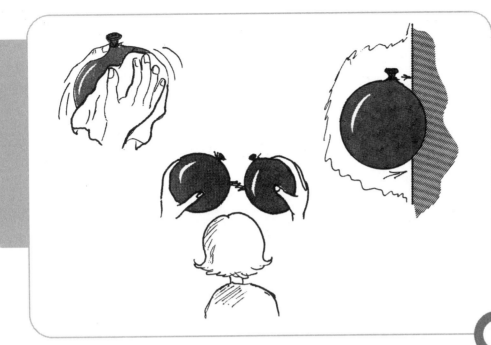

PRINCIPLES

Electricity can be made, and static electricity can be seen.

SCIENCE EXPERIENCE

- ○ Blow up the balloons. Rub one balloon briskly on their hair or a piece of wool. Push the balloon against the wall.
- ○ Explain to the children that static electricity created by rubbing the balloon on the wool causes the balloon to stick to the wall.
- ○ Tell the children that they can also see this static electricity. Ask if they have ever been shocked after walking on a carpet or putting on a sweater. Tell them they can see what this looks like when it is dark.
- ○ Darken the room and rub both balloons briskly on the wool. Hold the balloons, almost touching, so the children can observe a spark jump between them.
- ○ Encourage the children to explore the materials.

MATERIALS

two balloons
wool cloth
dark room

WORDS TO DISCUSS

spark
static electricity

EXPLANATION

Static electricity is created when certain objects rub together, like the balloon and the wool. A spark occurs when two objects that have static electricity in them come together.

Static Electricity

MATERIALS

piece of wool
balloons
comb
small pieces of paper

WORDS TO DISCUSS

attract
friction
magnet
produce
static electricity
wool

SCIENCE EXPERIENCE

○ Let the children blow up balloons.
○ Ask the children to put their balloons against the wall to see if they will stick.
○ Rub the balloons on the wool. See if they stick.
○ Explain that static electricity builds when you rub the balloon on wool, and that the electricity makes the balloon stick to the wall.
○ Using a pocket comb, ask a child to comb her hair when it is very dry. Then ask the child to use the comb as if it were a magnet to pick up small pieces of paper. "What happens? Why?"

EXPLANATION

Static electricity builds up to make objects attract or push away from each other. Static in a child's hair, created by running the comb through it, makes it stand up.

40

On Charting Temperature

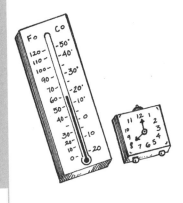

DATE	8:00 AM	2:00 PM	DATE	8:00 AM	2:00 PM
Feb. 1	30°	40°	Feb. 16		
2	33°	45°	17		
3	28°	34°	18		
4	26°	32°	19		
5	31°	45°	20		
6	35°	49°	21		
7	43°	55°	22		
8	34°	45°	23		
9	35°	43°	24		
10	28°	35°	25		
11	34°	40°	26		
12	39°	52°	27		
13	40°	59°	28		
14					
15					

Temperature can be measured with a thermometer. Temperature changes from day to day as well as during the day.

SCIENCE EXPERIENCE

- Introduce the children to the thermometer.
- Practice with them until they can read the temperature.
- Using poster board, make a chart to record the temperature daily at specified times. Let the children take turns recording the temperatures each morning and each afternoon.

MATERIALS

large thermometer
piece of poster board

WORDS TO DISCUSS

Celsius
Centigrade
Fahrenheit
temperature
thermometer

EXPLANATION

Different scales are used to record temperature in Centigrade (or Celsius) and Fahrenheit. Each scale measures temperature differently. Mark the thermometer at 32°F (0°C) and talk about water freezing at that temperature. Mark the thermometer at 212°F (100°C) and talk about water boiling at that temperature.

41

Parachute Game

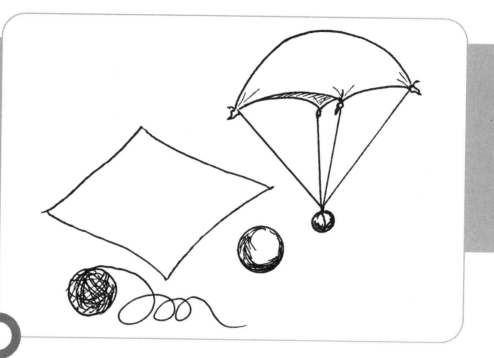

PRINCIPLES

Air, even though we don't normally see it, is an object itself. Air affects the way objects behave.

MATERIALS

small ball
string
two-foot square of cloth

WORDS TO DISCUSS

parachute

SCIENCE EXPERIENCE

- Allow the children to throw the ball into the air and catch it.
- Tell the children that if they had a way to catch some of the air, it would make a difference in the way the ball fell.
- Tie a string around the ball and tie the string to the four corners of the cloth. Fold the cloth and throw the cloth and ball into the air. The parachute should float down.
- Let the children try throwing the parachute.

NOTE: Try this outdoors so the children can throw the ball without the danger of hurting another child or breaking something.

EXPLANATION

The cloth will fill with air. Since air is an object, it will cause the parachute to fall slowly.

42

Night and Day

SCIENCE EXPERIENCE

- Talk about the different things children do during the day and night.
- Mark a circle on the floor with tape.
- Turn out the lights in the room. Tell the children to gather in a circle to represent the earth.
- Select one child to be the sun, and ask this child to stand holding a flashlight toward the circle.
- Have the "Earth" walk in a circle. When children are in the light, they can march, sing, dance, or pretend to do other things that people do during the day, like read a book. When they are not in the light, they put their heads down and walk quietly, like people sleeping.

MATERIALS

flashlight
masking tape

WORDS TO DISCUSS

day
Earth
night
rotate
sun

EXPLANATION

Talk about differences in night and day. Tell the children that as the Earth rotates, half of the earth is in the sun and the other half is dark, causing day and night.

Learning About the Sun

PRINCIPLES

The sun gives us light and heat. Sunlight can burn.

BLACK PAPER

MATERIALS

thermometer
magnifying glass
black construction paper

WORDS TO DISCUSS

energy
heat
light
sunburn
sunscreen
sunny
ultraviolet radiation
warm

SCIENCE EXPERIENCE

- Discuss the change the sun makes in our skin color over the course of the summer. Why? Talk about the heat given off by the sun. Talk about the shade and the difference in temperature.
- Talk about being sunburned. Let one child explain to the other children what it is like to be sunburned.
- Talk about sunscreen and why it is important.
- Go outside on a warm, sunny day. Stand in the sun and feel the heat. "Why does your skin feel warm?" Stand in the shade. "Is there a difference? Why?"
- Leave one piece of black construction paper inside, and keep one outside in the sun when it is not raining. "Is there a difference in color? Why?"

EXPLANATION

Sunlight is hot because it is full of energy, which makes things hot. We use sunglasses and sunscreen to protect our skin from being burned by the ultraviolet radiation in sunlight. The sun's UV radiation can also be harmful to other objects, such as paper. Sunlight can change the color of construction paper.

44

Rotation of the Earth

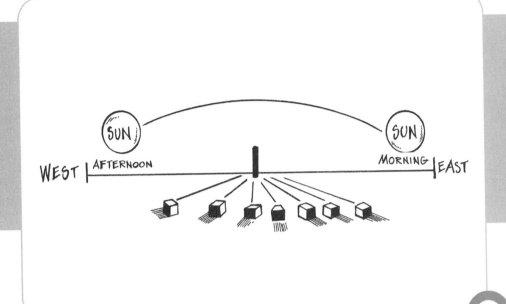

PRINCIPLES

The sun shines from different directions during the day. The Earth rotates.

SCIENCE EXPERIENCE

- Talk to the children about how the sun rises in the east and sets in the west. Demonstrate by rotating the globe next to the ball.

- On the playground, set up a stick in the morning so it casts a shadow. Let the children mark the end of the shadow with a small block. Let them use other blocks to mark the end of the shadow each hour.

- Ask the children questions. "Why did the shadows change?" "When was the shadow longest?" "When was the shadow shortest?"

MATERIALS

globe
ball to represent the sun
small wooden blocks
   for markers
stick

WORDS TO DISCUSS

globe
hour
longest
rotate
shadow
shortest

EXPLANATION

Tell the children that light moves in a straight line. If you look at a shadow, you can tell where the light is coming from. You can also tell the time of day. When the sun is lower, shadows are longer; when the sun is higher, shadows are shorter.

45

Dressing for the Seasons

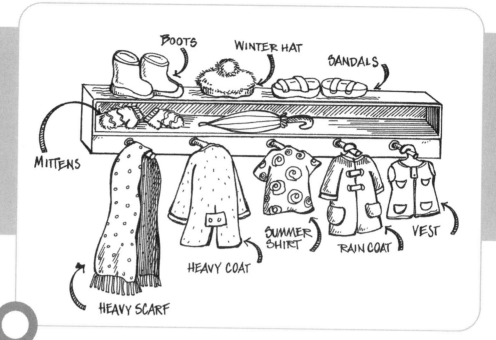

MATERIALS

An assortment of dress-up clothes and accessories, including heavy and light coats, raincoats, sweaters, shorts, short-sleeve shirts, gloves, snow boots, full-length mirror, hand mirror

WORDS TO DISCUSS

the seasons: Spring, Summer, Fall, Winter
breezy
chilly
freezing
hot
icy cold
warm

SCIENCE EXPERIENCE

○ Talk about hot, cold, cool, and warm weather. Talk about the seasons and the temperatures associated with each season. Talk about textures and weights of clothes.

○ Arrange the seasonal clothes in the dramatic play area on racks or clothes trees. Put footwear together, hats together, and so on.

○ Divide the children into four groups. Ask each group to dress as they would dress in one of the four seasons: Spring, Summer, Fall, Winter.

○ Let each group explain why they dressed the way they did. Have the children observe the different textures and weights of the clothes.

EXPLANATION

Our bodies must stay at a certain temperature in order to be healthy. When it is cold, our bodies need help to stay warm. Heavier, thicker materials like wool keep people from getting too cold. When it is hot out, people wear lighter clothes to stay cool.

46

Seasons

SCIENCE EXPERIENCE

- Talk about the weather. "What is the season?" "What kind of clothes are appropriate for each season?" "How do these clothes differ?" "Why do we wear heavy clothes in winter?" Ask questions and discuss each season and the clothing worn in that season.
- Help the children make a seasonal poster. Using a piece of poster board divided into four squares, label each square for a different season and paste a picture appropriate to the season next to the label.
- Let the children use catalogs and magazines to find pictures of different types of clothing. Ask them to cut out the pictures and paste them on the appropriate block.

MATERIALS

old catalogs
magazines
scissors
glue
poster board

WORDS TO DISCUSS

seasons

EXPLANATION

Making a visual representation of the seasons by the clothing of that season helps children understand that the weather changes with the seasons, since they already have a feeling for the way people dress in different weather.

47

Gravity

PRINCIPLES

*Gravity pulls objects
toward the Earth.*

MATERIALS

An assortment of small
   items such as a block,
   a pencil, scissors, toys

WORDS TO DISCUSS

fall
gravity
ground
hold

SCIENCE EXPERIENCE

○ Use the word "gravity" as you talk about objects falling. A young child
   can easily understand that whatever is dropped will fall. However, it is a
   stretch to expect the very young child to explain why. We can lay the
   foundation of future understanding.

○ Use the falling of a block structure as a learning experience. Ask
   questions after you drop the block. "Which way did it fall?" "If you drop a
   pencil, will it fall up or down?" "Will it ever fall to the side?"

○ Drop several objects to the floor such as a block, pencil, scissors, or toy.
   "Which ones fall up and which ones fall down?"

○ Have the children stretch out an arm to hold a small wooden block at
   shoulder height. Ask them to notice their arms getting tired as they hold
   the block. Explain that gravity is a force that can't be seen but can be
   felt as it pulls objects to the ground.

EXPLANATION

*Gravity is a force that pulls objects toward each other. The
bigger the object, the more gravity it has. The Earth is so large
that it pulls everything down toward it. Explain that this is
why when the children jump, they come right back down, and
why things never fall up or to the side.*

48

Using a Balance Scale

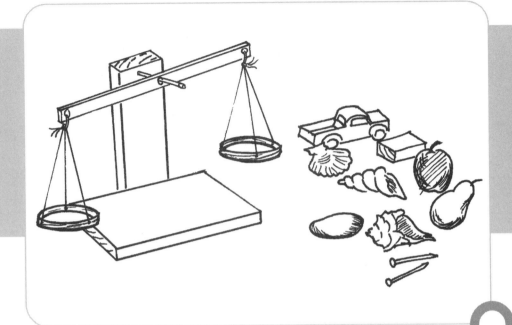

Objects have different weights. Objects may be classified according to weight.

SCIENCE EXPERIENCE

- ○ Introduce the children individually or in small groups to the balance scale.
- ○ After the children have become familiar with the scale, allow them to compare weights and sizes of various objects.
- ○ Let the children select one object and sort the remaining objects according to which are heavier, lighter, or weigh the same as the chosen object.

MATERIALS

simple balance scale
an assortment of objects
  to be weighed

WORDS TO DISCUSS

balance
heavier
lighter
same
scale
sort
weigh
weight

EXPLANATION

Because gravity pulls on objects differently depending on how much matter each contains, some objects are lighter and other objects are heavier.

49

Magnets

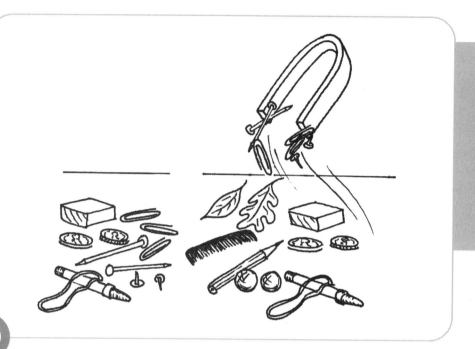

MATERIALS

large magnet
several different objects
   made of different
   materials
two plastic produce or
   meat trays

WORDS TO DISCUSS

attract
magnet
magnetism
metal
repel

SCIENCE EXPERIENCE

- Encourage the children to spread the different objects out on a table.
- Let them explore with the magnet to see which objects it will pick up and which it won't pick up. "What will it pick up?" "Will it pick up everything?" "Why not?" "Does it have anything to do with what the object is made of?"
- Encourage the children to sort objects into labeled trays according to whether or not they attract the magnet.
- Discuss the materials that the magnet will attract and materials that it will not attract. Predict which materials in the classroom may be attracted to the magnet. Test to see if the guesses are correct.

EXPLANATION

Magnets will only pick up objects that are attracted to magnets, meaning some metals.

50

Growing Crystals

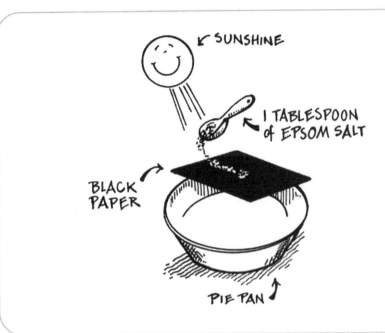

SUNSHINE

1 TABLESPOON
of EPSOM SALT

BLACK
PAPER

PIE PAN

PRINCIPLES

Crystals are formed when liquids turn into solids.

SCIENCE EXPERIENCE

- Create Epsom salt crystals.
  - Use an old pie pan or shallow glass bowl; put black construction paper in the bottom.
  - Add one tablespoon of Epsom salt to one-quarter cup of warm water. Stir until the salt is dissolved.
  - Pour the salty water onto the black paper in the pie pan.
  - Put the pie pan out in the sun. When the water evaporates, the children will see lots of crystal spikes on the black paper.

- Create sugar crystals.
CAUTION: The pan and sugar solution will be very hot; this activity should be carefully supervised.
  - Put half a cup of tap water in the pan.
  - Heat the water over a flame. Bring the water to a boil. Pour the sugar into the water and stir. Keep adding more until it will no longer dissolve. Then add just a little more water and continue to heat and stir until all of the material disappears.
  - Turn off the burner and let the water cool to room temperature.
  - Pour the contents into the cup. Put the cup somewhere where it will not be disturbed until the liquid evaporates. This could take several weeks.

MATERIALS

black construction paper
scissors
pie pan, cake pan, or
    shallow bowl
warm water
Epsom salt (usually near
    rubbing alcohol in the
    supermarket)
plastic or paper cup
1 cup sugar
pan for heating water
source of heat for water
optional: pencil, string,
    and weight (like a small
    metal nut or washer)

WORDS TO DISCUSS

crystal
salt
solution
additional information on
    crystals from the library

51

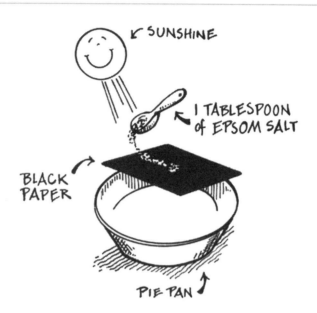

- When you check the cup after all the liquid is gone, you should see crystals coating the sides and bottoms of the cups. If you made both sugar and salt crystals, notice that they form different shapes.
- Optional: variation of the above activity will give you larger and more regularly-shaped crystals.
  - Tie a string to the middle of a pencil and tie a weight to the other end of the string. Make sure the distance between the weight and the pencil is less than the depth of the cup.
  - Put the pencil across the top of the cup so the string and weight hang in the cup. Crystals will form on the string as the liquid evaporates.

EXPLANATION

When you add Epsom salt or sugar to water, they will dissolve. When you leave the pan or cup, the water evaporates and the salt or sugar forms crystals shaped like long needles. If you try this with table salt instead of Epsom salt, you will not get crystal spikes because table salt and Epsom salt are chemically different, so the crystals they form are also different.

Environment

A, B, Cedar: An Alphabet of Trees by George Ella Lyon

Any Room for Me? by Loek Koopmans

Bedtime for Frances by Russell Hoban

The Berenstain Bears Don't Pollute by Jan and Stan Berenstain

Connections: Finding Out About the Environment by David Suzuki

Everybody Needs a Rock by Byrd Baylor

Flash, Crash, Rumble, and Roll by Franklyn M. Branley

Frog and Toad Together by Arnold Lobel

A House Is a House for Me by Mary Ann Hoberman

How Do You Know It's Fall? by Allan Fowler

How Do You Know It's Summer? by Allan Fowler

I Can Tell By Touching by Carolyn Otto

Is This a House for Hermit Crab? By Megan McDonald

My Visit to the Dinosaurs by Aliki

Papa, Please Get the Moon for Me by Eric Carle

The Planets by Gail Gibbons

The Planets in Our Solar System by Franklyn M. Branley

Recycle! A Handbook for Kids by Gail Gibbons

Recycle Every Day by Nancy Elizabeth Wallace

Science Play! by Jill Frankel Hauser

Sense Suspense: A Guessing Game for the Five Senses by Bruce McMillan

Stone Soup by Ann McGovern

Storms by Seymour Simon

The Story of Light by Susan L. Roth

The Sun (Planet Library) by Robin Kerrod

The Sun Is Always Shining Somewhere by Allan Fowler

Sun Up, Sun Down by Gail Gibbons

The Sun's Family of Planets by Allan Fowler

What Is a Magnet? by Jim Pipe

What Magnets Can Do by Allan Fowler

What Makes Day and Night? by Franklyn M. Branley

What Makes a Magnet? by Franklyn M. Branley

What Makes a Shadow? by Clyde Robert Bulla

What's Out There? A Book About Space by Lynn Wilson

Where Once There Was a Wood by Denise Fleming

54

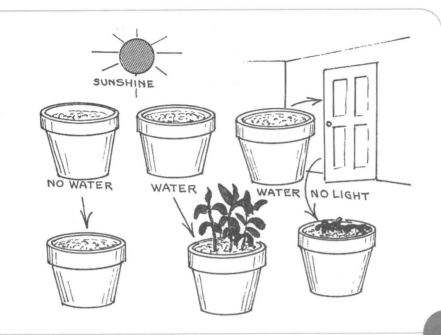

Experiences With
Plants

Seed Party

Growing Without Seeds

Planting Beans

Growing Beans

Development

Making a Seed Book

Children's Garden

Seeds and Fruits

Children's Books

Seed Party

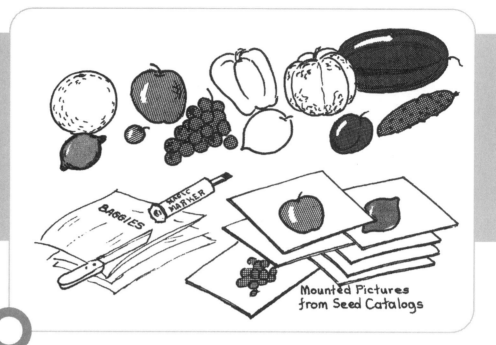

Mounted Pictures from Seed Catalogs

PRINCIPLES

Plants produce seeds that, in turn, produce plants. Different plants have different seeds.

MATERIALS

assortment of fruits such as orange, apple, lemon, cantaloupe, small watermelon, peach, cherry
plastic sandwich bags
marker
pictures of fruit cut from magazines

WORDS TO DISCUSS

alike
different
grow
plant
pulp
reproduce
seed
skin

SCIENCE EXPERIENCE

- Let the children take turns carefully cutting the fruits and taking out seeds. Supervise as needed.
- Talk about differences in seeds and plants. Discuss plant growth and what is necessary to grow healthy plants. Talk about seeds that are eaten and those that are not eaten. Children may want to plant some of their seeds.
- Talk about how the seeds are alike and how they are different. Put the different seeds into plastic sandwich bags and label accordingly. Later, match the seeds to the pictures.
- If you extend this activity over several days, the children can enjoy the fruit at snack time or make a fruit salad. This activity may also be done using vegetables. There are many seed catalogs with beautiful pictures.

EXPLANATION

Plants produce seeds because that is how they reproduce (make more plants). For example, if a peach falls from a tree, the seed inside may grow into a new peach tree.

56

Growing Without Seeds

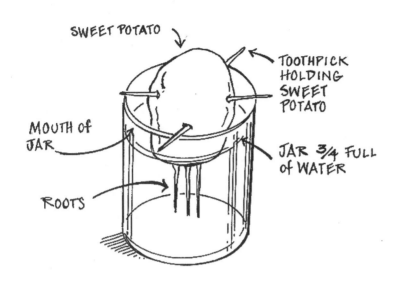

SWEET POTATO

TOOTHPICK HOLDING SWEET POTATO

MOUTH of JAR

JAR 3/4 FULL of WATER

ROOTS

SCIENCE EXPERIENCE

- Fill a jar about three-quarters full of water and place a sweet potato in the water so only the bottom third of the potato is in the water. Toothpicks put into the potato and laid across the mouth of the jar will keep the potato from slipping further into the water.
- Cut the top off of a carrot that has already had the greens removed.
- Place the carrot top in a shallow dish of water, flat side down.
- Observe that both plants produce roots and leaves.

MATERIALS

A variety of plants that will root themselves in water, such as sweet potatoes, carrots, or vines

WORDS TO DISCUSS

leaves
plant
roots
underground
water

EXPLANATION

Some plants grow from seeds and some from cuttings. Potatoes sprout roots which grow into more potatoes. These roots are called tubers, and potatoes are called tuber vegetables.

57

Planting Beans

Sunlight and water are necessary for plants to grow.

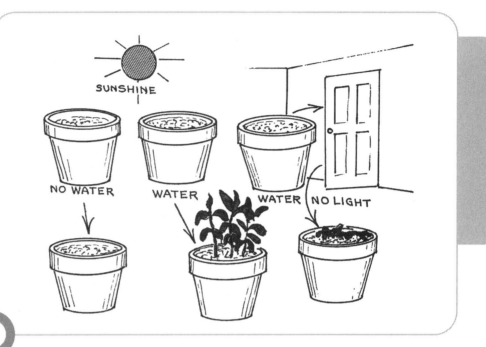

MATERIALS

three flower pots
nine dried beans
soil mixture of ½ potting
   soil, ¼ garden soil,
   ¼ sand

WORDS TO DISCUSS

die
grow
growth
plants
soil
sunlight
water
wilt

SCIENCE EXPERIENCE

○ Talk with the children about how plants grow and the help they need to grow. Be sure to discuss both sunlight and water. Explain to the children that together you will determine if sunshine and water are necessary for growing plants.

○ Fill three flower pots with a good soil mixture. Children should help you mix the soil. Plant three beans in each pot. Put two pots on the window ledge so they both get sun.

○ Keep the soil in one pot moistened so that it does not dry out. Do not add water to the second pot.

○ Put the third pot in the closet where it will not get sunshine and keep the soil moist.

○ Observe the growth of the plants. Talk about what happens when plants do not receive water. Talk about what happens when plants do not receive sunlight.

EXPLANATION

Plants need food to survive, just like people and animals. Sunlight helps plants make food. Plants also need water just like people and animals. Without sun or water, plants cannot grow.

58

Growing Beans

PRINCIPLES

Seeds germinate, sprout, and grow into adult plants.

SCIENCE EXPERIENCE

- Give each child a baby food or another type of jar.
- Put a strip of tape with the child's name on each jar. Older children may write their own names.
- Fill each jar about one-quarter full with cotton.
- In each jar, put two beans between the cotton and the glass and two beans on top of the cotton.
- Dampen the cotton and keep it damp.
- Place the jars on the window ledge so they receive light. Watch what happens! Talk about the sprouting of the beans, and the growing of roots as well as other parts of the plant.

MATERIALS

small glass jars (baby food jars are excellent)
masking tape
lima beans or other varieties of beans
cotton
water

WORDS TO DISCUSS

cotton
damp
germinate
light
sprout
water
wet

EXPLANATION

Plants go through stages as they grow from seeds to full-grown plants. They must sprout roots to grow; this is called germination. Then the stem and leaves can start to grow. Lima beans are seeds from a lima bean plant.

59

Development

Plants and animals go through a sequence of stages in growth.

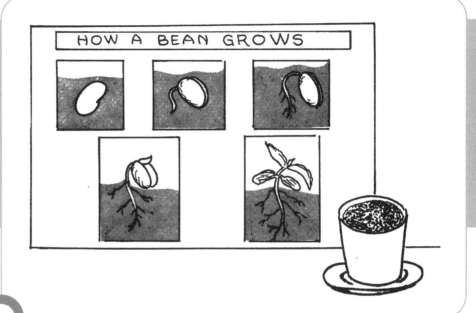

HOW A BEAN GROWS

MATERIALS

series of pictures showing the development of a plant from a seed

series of pictures showing the development of an animal from an egg (chicken, frog)

WORDS TO DISCUSS

baby
development
grow
old
seed
sequence
stage
young

SCIENCE EXPERIENCE

○ Use one example (plants or animals) at a time. It is probably best to begin with plants.

○ Talk about plants developing from seeds. Compare and contrast animals and plants.

○ Make a bulletin board of the pictures in the correct sequence. Talk daily about the development.

○ Let the children tell the story of the development.

○ Code the pictures with numbers on the back. Put the pictures in random order on the chalk ledge. Allow different children to put the pictures in sequence.

EXPLANATION

All living things develop and grow in a sequence of stages. Plants grow from small seeds to sprouts to big plants just as chickens grow from small eggs to baby chicks to big chickens.

60

Making a Seed Book

PRINCIPLES

Each plant makes its own type of seed. We can match plants with their seeds.

SCIENCE EXPERIENCE

- Let each child construct a seed book using a piece of construction paper as the cover.
- Lay two pieces of manila paper on top of the construction paper, fold in half, and staple on the folded edge.
- Collect seeds and/or leaves from plants that grow outside.
- Or, collect seeds and glue them to a page along with a picture of the plant from a seed catalog or magazine.
- Label each page with the name of the plant and help the child with notes or observations she might wish to add.

MATERIALS

construction paper
manila paper
stapler
marker
glue
scissors
old seed catalogs
magazines

WORDS TO DISCUSS

develop
grow
plants
matching
seeds
sprout

EXPLANATION

When given the right environment, seeds will grow into plants. Seeing pictures of seeds with the plants they become helps children associate plants with seeds.

61

Children's Garden

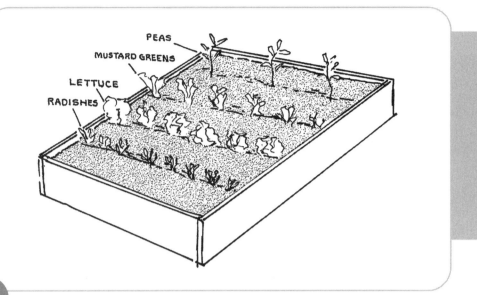

PEAS
MUSTARD GREENS
LETTUCE
RADISHES

PRINCIPLES

Plants are a positive and important part of life. They can be fun to care for, and provide food.

MATERIALS

plastic or metal dishpan or a shallow wooden box (be sure to make a hole in the bottom of the container)
potting soil
sand
variety of garden seeds (mustard greens, radishes, lettuce, peas, kale, and others)

WORDS TO DISCUSS

mixing soil
names of vegetables such as carrot and broccoli
planting
tending

SCIENCE EXPERIENCE

- This is an indoor activity because many schools do not have space that may be used for a garden. For schools that have outside space, this is a good outdoor activity.
- Explain to interested children what they can do. Let them help mix the soil with half potting soil, a quarter sand, and a quarter garden soil that they dig for themselves outside.
- Prepare the soil and talk with the children about what should be planted and why. Try to follow the children's suggestions on what to plant.
- Tending the garden is fulfilling as a long-term project. Children are proud of plants they helped to grow.
- Plants can be started indoors and transferred outside when ready. If there is room outdoors, children can plant popcorn in the fall to be harvested after the first frost. Children love to rub two ears together to remove kernels from the cobs. Pop the kernels, and the children can enjoy a favorite snack.

EXPLANATION

Many plants produce foods that are essential for people, such as corn, wheat, apples, and carrots. Farmers plant gardens and care for the plants to make sure they grow properly, so people will have food to eat.

Seeds and Fruits

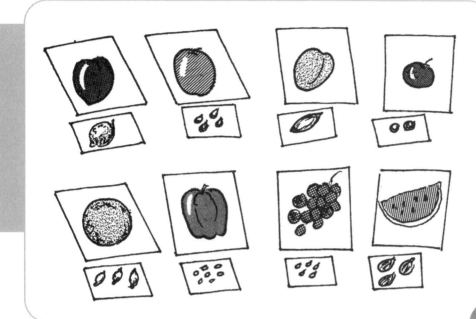

PRINCIPLES

Fruits, vegetables, and all plants grow from seeds. Fruits have different names and different-looking seeds.

SCIENCE EXPERIENCE

- Let the children cut pictures of fruits and plants from seed catalogs. Mount the pictures on a piece of poster board.
- Ask the children to bring in seeds that match the pictures.
- Purchase seeds that children might have difficulty finding.
- Mount the seeds on small pieces of cardboard and keep them in the science center so the children can match the seeds with the pictures.
- It may be difficult for young children to match seeds with plants, especially if they are alike. Supply a variety of very different plants and seeds for this activity (apple, lima bean, watermelon, peach, avocado).

MATERIALS

scissors
seed catalogs
glue
poster board

WORDS TO DISCUSS

bean
core
names of plants and
   fruits
pit
seed

EXPLANATION

Seeds come in all shapes and sizes, and have different names, such as a "pit" or a "bean." Despite their differences, all seeds grow into plants.

Plants

Children's Books

Chrysanthemum by Kevin Henkes

Crinkleroot's Guide to Knowing the Trees by Jim Arnosky

The Empty Pot by Demi

Eating the Alphabet: Fruits and Vegetables from A to Z by Lois Ehlert

First Comes Spring by Anne F. Rockwell

Flower Garden by Eve Bunting

Flowers by Ivan Anatta

Fresh Fall Leaves by Betsy Franco

From Seed to Plant by Gail Gibbons

From Seed to Sunflower by Gerald Legg

The Giving Tree by Shel Silverstein

Growing Vegetable Soup by Lois Ehlert

Have You Seen Trees? by Joanne Oppenheim

How Do Apples Grow? by Betsy Maestro

It Could Still Be a Flower by Allan Fowler

It Could Still Be a Tree by Allan Fowler

Jack's Garden by Henry Cole

Look What I Did With a Leaf by Morteza E. Sohi

One Bean by Anne F. Rockwell

Pick, Pull, Snap! Where Once a Flower Bloomed by Lola M. Schaefer

Plants! by Andrew Haslam

Plants That Never Ever Bloom by Ruth Heller

Planting a Rainbow by Lois Ehlert

The Reason for a Flower by Ruth Heller

Red Leaf, Yellow Leaf by Lois Ehlert

The Seasons of Arnold's Apple Tree by Gail Gibbons

A Seed Grows: My First Look at a Plant's Life Cycle by Pamela Hickman

This Year's Garden by Cynthia Rylant

The Tiny Seed by Eric Carle

What's This? by Caroline Mockford

A Tree Is Nice by Janice May Udry

Trees of North America by Christian Frank Brockman

Vegetables, Vegetables by Fay Robinson and Allan Fowler

The Wheat We Eat by Allan Fowler

Why Do Leaves Change Color? by Besty Maestro

Experiences With the
Senses

Washing and Feeling

Sounds Around Us

Music Everywhere

Hello, Who's There?

Tasting

What Is That Smell?

Exploring Odors

Touching

Children's Books

Washing and Feeling

MATERIALS

warm water
doll clothes
liquid soap
clothesline

WORDS TO DISCUSS

dry
drying
feel
soap
soapy
touch
wash

SCIENCE EXPERIENCE

- Let the children gather up the doll clothes in the housekeeping center.
- Encourage the children to wash all the clothes.
- First, wash in plain water. "How does it feel?" "Do the clothes feel different?"
- Now let the children use liquid soap on them.
- Rinse the clothes. "How do they feel?" Hang them on a line. "How do they feel as they begin to dry?"
- Discuss the different ways the clothes feel, why we wash clothes, why we use soap, and why we hang clothes on a clothesline.

EXPLANATION

Touching objects helps children become familiar with them. It is important to explain touch to children because it works together with sight to help children identify and understand objects in their world. They can tell if clothes are wet, dry, or soapy with the sense of touch. Soap is made of a substance (a base, or alkali) that makes skin feel slippery.

66

Sounds Around Us

SCIENCE EXPERIENCE

- Listening is a learned skill. The first step in teaching listening is to make children aware of sounds. Take turns with a group or with an individual, asking each child to close his eyes.
- Wad up the paper while his eyes are closed. Ask the child to identify the sound.
- Repeat using other objects.

MATERIALS

paper
chalk
pen
zipper
jar with screw lid
bell
book
other objects that make noise

WORDS TO DISCUSS

loud
quiet
sharp
soft
sounds

EXPLANATION

This activity is designed to make children aware that different things have sounds of their own, and that they can recognize the sounds with their ears and the sense of hearing.

67

Music Everywhere

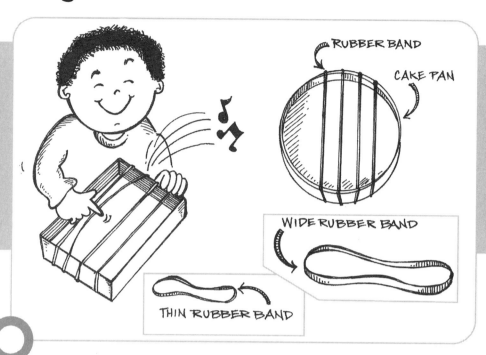

RUBBER BAND
CAKE PAN
WIDE RUBBER BAND
THIN RUBBER BAND

PRINCIPLES

Sounds can be produced by vibrations.

MATERIALS

square cake pan or boxes
assorted rubber bands

WORDS TO DISCUSS

loud
soft
sound
thin
vibrate
wide

SCIENCE EXPERIENCE

- Place the rubber bands around the cake pan or box.
- Pluck each rubber band and watch it vibrate.
- Discuss with the children what happens. "Does the vibration have anything to do with the sound?" "How do the rubber bands vibrate to make a loud sound?" "How do they vibrate to make a soft sound?" "Does the width of the rubber band have anything to do with the sound it makes? What?"

EXPLANATION

The length of the rubber band, the width of the rubber band, and the placement of the rubber band on the pan determine the sound produced. The vibration of the rubber band causes the sound. Thick rubber bands produce lower sounds because they vibrate more slowly, and thin rubber bands vibrate more rapidly, causing a higher sound.

68

Hello, Who's There?

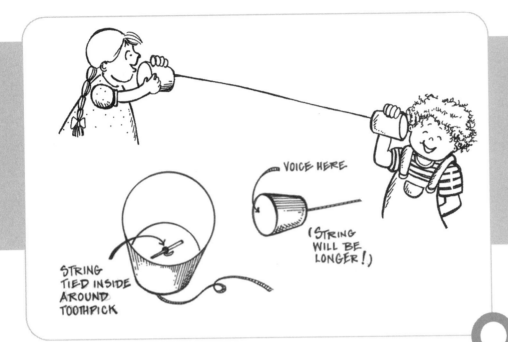

VOICE HERE

(STRING WILL BE LONGER!)

STRING TIED INSIDE AROUND TOOTHPICK

PRINCIPLES

Sound travels through the air and through objects.

SCIENCE EXPERIENCE

- Punch a small hole in the center of the bottom of each plastic cup.
- Insert the string through the hole in the plastic cup from the outside to the inside.
- Tie the end of the string inside the cup around a toothpick and pull. The toothpick will lie across the bottom of the cup, preventing the string from falling out.
- Do the same with the other cup and the other end of the string.
- Pull the string tight between the two cups.
- Let one child speak directly into the cup while holding the cup with both hands. The other child listens, holding the side of her cup with both hands. "What happens?" "How does the sound travel?" "What happens if the string is not tight?"

MATERIALS

two plastic Styrofoam cups
long string
two toothpicks

WORDS TO DISCUSS

cup
ear
hear
hold
inside
listen
mouth
outside
speak
string
tight

EXPLANATION

The sound travels along the string when it is tight.

Tasting

PRINCIPLES

Taste is one of our senses. We can distinguish between substances with this sense.

MATERIALS

foods that are salty, sweet, sour, bitter, spicy, and bland
carrots
pickle slices
cheese cubes
radishes
raisins
grapefruit juice
milk, whole or chocolate

WORDS TO DISCUSS

bitter
bland
crispy
hard
salty
shape
soft
sour
spicy
sweet
taste

SCIENCE EXPERIENCE

○ Have a tasting party to acquaint the children with different tastes.
○ Talk about how the food tastes, and about the texture, appearance, and other features of the food. "How is each food different?" "Do they feel different?" "How are they alike?"

EXPLANATION

People can tell which foods are good and which are bad with their sense of taste. The tongue is covered with little taste buds that sense how things taste: sour, sweet, salty, or bitter.

70

What Is That Smell?

PRINCIPLES

Different things have different smells. We can use smells to identify substances. Smell is one of our five senses.

SCIENCE EXPERIENCE

- Put a wadded-up paper towel in the bottom of each baby food jar.
- Put a different object for smelling in each jar.
- Allow the children, while blindfolded, to smell and guess what the odors are.
- Talk about the different smells. "How are they alike and how are they different?"

MATERIALS

clean baby food jars
paper towels
vanilla extract
lemon extract
cloves
mustard
fried bacon
onions

WORDS TO DISCUSS

blindfold
odor
guess
smell

EXPLANATION

Tell the children that smell rises from the jars into the air. Smells are composed of elements that are too small to see. Though smells can't be seen, noses are made to sense odors and to tell whether something smells good, bad, or has no odor.

71

Exploring Odors

PRINCIPLES

Almost everything has an odor that can be detected through our sense of smell.

MATERIALS

variety of objects
usually found in the
classroom

WORDS TO DISCUSS

classify
different
odor
smell

SCIENCE EXPERIENCE

○ Divide the children into pairs and let them take an "odor walk" around the room.

○ Encourage them to smell objects they wouldn't expect to smell, such as leather, blocks, paint, tables, rugs, pet cages, painted objects, and sinks.

○ Talk about what they have smelled. Classify objects into categories such as "smells good," "smells bad," "doesn't smell much," or "smells like..."

○ Talk about how different things smell different and why they smell different.

EXPLANATION

Odors are made of little particles called odor particles that noses can smell. Animals and plants and products made from them have the strongest odors. For example, the glass in the window has very little odor, whereas a peanut butter and jelly sandwich has a strong smell. Even books, made from trees, have a unique odor.

72

Touching

BURLAP SANDPAPER SILK CLAY PAPER

PRINCIPLES

Touch is one of our basic senses. We can identify objects by the way they feel.

SCIENCE EXPERIENCE

- Lay the objects out so the children can handle them and talk about them.
- Talk about the way each object feels. Introduce vocabulary.
- Put the objects in a bag. Let each child put his or her hand into the bag and select an object by feel.
- Ask the child to describe the object. "Is it hard? Soft? Rough? Smooth?" Let the child guess what the object is without looking at it.

MATERIALS

textured objects such as sandpaper, silk, burlap, clay, metal, paper
any other readily available textured materials in the classroom

WORDS TO DISCUSS

hard
rough
smooth
soft

EXPLANATION *Talk about hands and how we use them. Explain that our fingers can touch, hold, and pick up objects. The skin all over our bodies feels things like texture and temperature. When a child picks up sandpaper, his skin feels that it is rough. When he picks up an ice cube, his skin feels that it is cold and wet.*

73

Senses

Early Morning in the Barn by Nancy Tafuri
Feeling Things by Allan Fowler
The Five Senses by Beth Sidel
The Five Senses by Keith Faulkner
My Five Senses by Aliki
Fuzzy Yellow Ducklings by Matthew Van Fleet
Hearing (The Library of the Five Senses and the Sixth Sense) by
    Sue Hurwitz
Hearing by Maria Rius
Hearing Sounds by Sally Hewitt
Hearing Things by Allan Fowler
Intuition (The Library of the Five Senses and the Sixth Sense) by
    Sue Hurwitz
Listen to the Rain by Bill Martin, Jr. and John Archambault
The Listening Walk by Paul Showers
Mama Don't Allow by Thacher Hurd
Night Sounds, Morning Colors by Rosemary Wells
Noises: Let's Learn by Anna Nilsen
Pots and Pans by Patricia Hubbell
Round and Square by Miriam Schlein
See, Hear, Touch, Taste, Smell by Melvin Berger
Sense It, Hear It by Maile and Wren
Sense It, See It by Maile and Wren
Sense It, Smell It by Maile and Wren
Sense It, Taste It by Maile and Wren
Sense It, Touch It by Maile and Wren
Sight (The Library of the Five Senses and the Sixth Sense) by
    Sue Hurwitz
Smell (The Library of the Five Senses and the Sixth Sense) by
    Sue Hurwitz
Smelling Things by Allan Fowler
Sounds All Around by Wendy Pfeffer
Taste (The Library of the Five Senses and the Sixth Sense) by
    Sue Hurwitz
Taste by Maria Rius
Touch (The Library of the Five Senses and the Sixth Sense) by
    Sue Hurwitz
Touch by Maria Rius
What Noise? by Debbie MacKinnon
Who's Making That Smell? by Jenny Tyler
You Can't Smell a Flower With Your Ear! by Joanna Cole
You Can't Taste a Pickle With Your Ear by Harriet Ziefert
Zin! Zin! Zin! A Violin by Lloyd Moss

Children's Books

(1)

sit 3 to 9 min.

(2)

ice cubes

(3)

Experiences With
Water

Making Steam

Making Clouds

Water and Ice

Water Trick

Floating Objects

Experimenting With Water

Evaporation

Making Frost

Fish Breathe

Children's Books

6

Making Steam

PRINCIPLES

Hot water changes to steam.

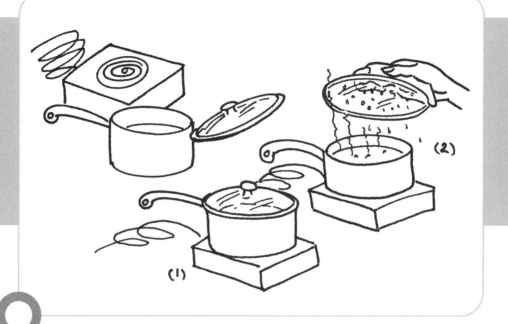

MATERIALS

hot plate
pan
glass lid that will fit
   completely over the
   top of the pan
water

WORDS TO DISCUSS

boil
steam
condensation

SCIENCE EXPERIENCE

- Explain to the children that they are going to do something different with water.
- Discuss how water turns into steam when it is boiled.
- Help the children fill the pan half full of water. Bring it to a boil on the hot plate. Be sure the glass is on the pan.
- When the water begins to boil, droplets of water will form on the inside of the glass lid. This is condensation. If desired, carefully lift the lid so the children can see the steam.

CAUTION: This activity must be closely supervised. Children must not attempt to touch the steam as severe burns can result.

EXPLANATION

Water turns to steam when it is heated to a certain temperature. Explain that the steam turns back to water as it cools and this causes the droplets of water to form, or condense, on the lid.

76

Making Clouds

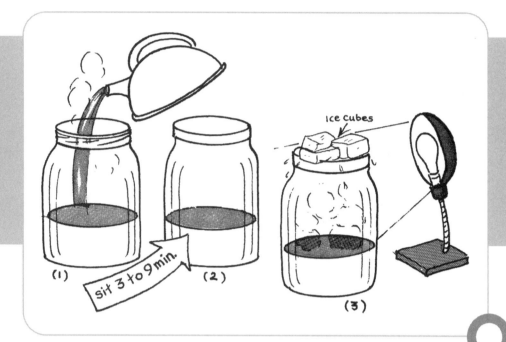

(1)   sit 3 to 9 min.   (2)

ice cubes

(3)

PRINCIPLES

Clouds are composed of water. Temperature affects cloud formation.

SCIENCE EXPERIENCE

- Pour two inches of very hot water into the glass container, put the lid on, and allow it to sit for three to nine minutes.
- Place ice cubes on the lid at the end of this time.
- Darken the room and hold a lamp behind the bottle. The children will observe the formation of a cloud inside the bottle.

CAUTION: Have the children watch from a safe distance. Glass can break and hot water can burn!

- Encourage the children to explore warm water and ice cubes in the sand and water table.

MATERIALS

Glass container with a wide mouth such as a restaurant–size mayonnaise or pickle jar
hot water
ice cubes
lamp
flat glass cover for glass container

WORDS TO DISCUSS

cloud formation
condensation
hot
ice cubes
moisture
steam
warm
water

EXPLANATION

As the ice cools the steam, clouds of moisture form. Real clouds form the same way. As moisture cools, it condenses and forms clouds.

77

Water and Ice

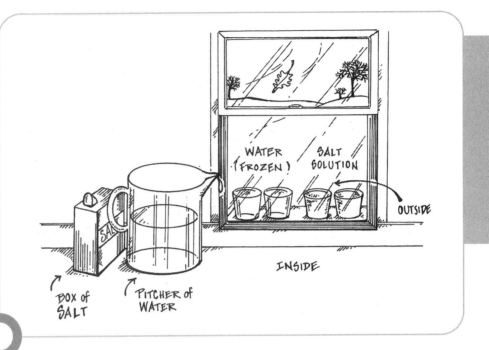

MATERIALS

paper cups
water
salt

WORDS TO DISCUSS

freeze
ice
melt

SCIENCE EXPERIENCE

○ An excellent time to experiment with ice is during freezing winter weather.

○ Fill several cups with water and two cups with a water-salt mixture. Mark each cup.

○ Set the cups outside on the window ledge at the end of the day to remain there overnight.

○ In the morning, bring in the cups. "What has happened?" "After the ice has melted, what is left?"

EXPLANATION

Most young children already associate cold weather with ice. Develop this further by explaining that it has to be a lot colder to freeze some liquids. If we add a liquid that is hard to freeze to water, it makes the water harder to freeze. Talk about antifreeze, and how it keeps cars from getting too cold to work in the winter.

Water Trick

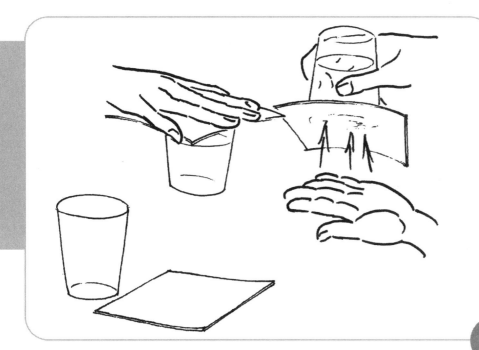

Air is real. Air can push and has weight.

SCIENCE EXPERIENCE

- Fill a glass with water. Turn the glass over and pour it out in the sink.
- Tell the children that you can turn the glass over without the water coming out. Let the children guess how you will do it.
- Fill your glass about three-quarters full with water and place the cardboard square over the mouth.
- Turn the glass over and the air will hold the cardboard in place and the water will remain in the glass. Talk to the children about how the air pushes on the cardboard.
- This will hold for only a short time. When the cardboard absorbs water it will fall off.
- Encourage the children to try this in the sand and water table.

MATERIALS

unbreakable glass
  of water
cardboard square large
  enough to cover the
  mouth of the glass

WORDS TO DISCUSS

air
cardboard
push
vacuum

EXPLANATION

When the glass is turned upside down, a partial vacuum is formed in the glass. As air tries to fill the vacuum, the air pressure put on the paper holds it in place.

Floating Objects

PRINCIPLES

Some objects will float on water, some will not.

MATERIALS

shallow pan of water
and assorted objects
made of different
materials
two plastic trays, one
with a picture of a
floating object and
the other with a
picture of a sinking
object

WORDS TO DISCUSS

density
float
heavier
lighter
matter
sink

SCIENCE EXPERIENCE

○ Fill a shallow pan with water.
○ Spread the objects you have collected on the table near the pan of water.
○ Encourage the children to experiment to see which objects float and which will not float. "Will all the objects float?"
○ Encourage the children to sort the objects into trays according to whether they float or don't float.
○ Ask the children why they think some objects float and some don't. Talk about the materials and what they are made of. Introduce the concept of density to the children. Compare the materials that float and sink for similarities and differences.

EXPLANATION

When objects float on water, they are less dense than the water. Density is the amount of matter in an object relative to its size. Things that are less dense are lighter than things that are more dense. A cork floats on the water because it is less dense, or has less matter, or "stuff," than water. A toy truck will sink because it is denser than water.

80

Experimenting With Water

PRINCIPLES

Water affects substances differently.

SCIENCE EXPERIENCE

○ Let the children explore the effect of water on different substances.

○ Fill the jars with water.

○ Put a tissue in one, sugar in another, salt in another, vegetable oil in another, a nail in another and a marble or rock in another.

○ Let the children observe what happens over a period of time.

○ Pour water through tubes and funnels of different sizes and observe the speed at which the water flows.

○ Pour water on several different textures of cloth.

○ Discuss the results. "Which items dissolve and which do not?" Rust forms on the nail. Water flows through tubes and funnels. Water has a different effect on different textures and substances.

MATERIALS

clear, unbreakable jars
water
tissues
sugar
salt
vegetable oil
nail and marble or rock
different textures of cloth
tubes and funnels of
   different sizes

WORDS TO DISCUSS

bubble
dissolve
flow
funnel
observe
rust
water

EXPLANATION

Water affects objects differently depending on what the objects are made of. Salt and sugar dissolve in water. A nail is made of iron, which rusts in water. Fabric is made of material that will absorb water.

Evaporation

MATERIALS

glass jar or shallow pan
water
marker

WORDS TO DISCUSS

evaporate
humidity
moisture
sediment

SCIENCE EXPERIENCE

- Place the glass jar or shallow pan in the science center.
- Fill the container three-quarters full of water. Mark the level of the water.
- Each day, mark the new level of water. In a few days, the water will be gone, leaving a small amount of sediment.

EXPLANATION

Water evaporates into the air. Talk about how water is absorbed into the air through evaporation. Talk about moisture and humidity. Call attention to the leftover sediment. Salts and other impurities are left after the water evaporates.

82

Making Frost

PRINCIPLES

Changes in temperature cause dew. Frost is frozen dew.

SCIENCE EXPERIENCE

- Let the children put two cups of crushed ice and one-half cup of rock salt in a can.
- Have the children stir the mixture rapidly. Move on to another activity and tell the children they will return to the can in thirty minutes.
- When you return, the outside of the can will have dew on it. Explain to the children that this is the same way dew forms on grass in the morning.
- If you wait a while longer, the dew will change to frost. Ask children if they have seen frost on grass, and explain that frost happens when dew forms and then freezes.

MATERIALS

tin can with lid removed
rock salt
crushed ice

WORDS TO DISCUSS

condensation
dew
freeze
frost
mix
mixture
outside
salt

EXPLANATION

Talk about where the dew came from and how it was formed, and talk about the dew changing to frost. As the can cools, the moisture in the air condenses on the cool surface. As the can becomes colder, the water on the surface of the can freezes, causing frost to form. This is how dew and frost form in nature, as well.

Fish Breathe

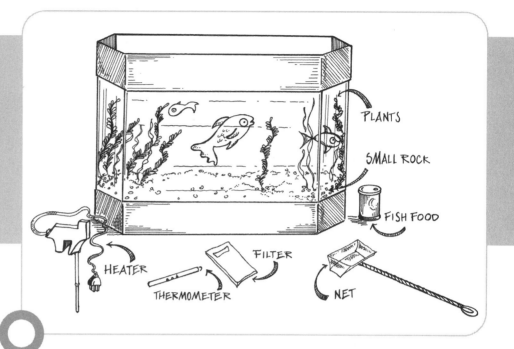

PLANTS

SMALL ROCK

FISH FOOD

HEATER

THERMOMETER

FILTER

NET

MATERIALS

fish tank
tank accessories
fish
fish food

WORDS TO DISCUSS

breathe
gills
lungs

SCIENCE EXPERIENCE

- Be sure the fish are properly cared for while children watch how they move and breathe.
- Point out the fish's gills to the children.
- Different children may be assigned the responsibility of feeding the fish and cleaning the tank, as necessary. Proper care of pets and plants is important and should be fully understood by children.
- Ask the children questions about the fish. "What are the fish doing?" "How do they swim? Eat? Sleep?"

EXPLANATION

Animals breathe because they need oxygen from the air to survive. Fish breathe water into their gills just as people breathe air into their lungs. Explain that the oxygen we get from the air when we breathe is the same that fish get from water when they breathe.

84

Water

Cloud Book by Julian May

The Cloud Book by Tomie dePaola

A Drop Around the World by Barbara Shaw McKinney

Follow the Water from Brook to Ocean by Arthur Dorros

I Am Water by Jean Marzollo

It Could Still Be a Lake by Allan Fowler

It Could Still Be Water by Allan Fowler

It's Raining, It's Pouring by Kin Eagle

Little Cloud by Eric Carle

The Magic School Bus: At the Water Works by Joanna Cole

The Magic School Bus Wet All Over: A Book About the Water Cycle
   by Patricia Reif

Rain by Peter Spier

Rain by Robert Kalan

Rain Drop Splash by Alvin Tresselt

The River by Mark Pollard

Sadie and the Snowman by Allen Morgan

Snow and Ice by Stephen Krensky

Snow Is Falling by Franklyn M. Branley

The Snowy Day by Ezra Jack Keats

We Need Water by Helen Frost

Water as a Gas by Helen Frost

Water as a Solid by Helen Frost

The Water Cycle by Helen Frost

Water, Water Everywhere by Mark J. Ranzon

What Do You See in a Cloud? by Allan Fowler

Where Do Puddles Go? by Fay Robinson

White Snow, Bright Snow by Alvin Tresselt

CUT OUT

PAPER SCRAPS

PASTE

MAGAZINES

FOOD BOOK

Miscellaneous Experiences

Learning About Transportation

Transportation

Roll on Big Wheels

Creating Colors

Collections

Food Book

Children's Books

Learning About Transportation

STICKS WITH STRING TIED to THEM (TO MARK OFF "STREET" IN GRASSY AREAS)

MATERIALS

small sticks

rags

ropes

tagboard

tricycles

wagons

whistle

cardboard police officer's
  badge

WORDS TO DISCUSS

traffic

road signs

SCIENCE EXPERIENCE

- Scratch a paved or dirt section of your playground to outline roads, or mark roadways with small sticks with bits of cloth tied onto the sticks on a grassy section.
- Make traffic signals from tagboard: Stop, Yield, Slow, Road Construction, No Right Turn.
- Appoint one child to be a traffic officer.
- After discussing the traffic signs and what they mean, let the children "travel the roads" on their tricycles and wagons.
- The traffic officer should be sure the signs are obeyed. The same physical setup may be used for a variety of games.

EXPLANATION *Talk about the meaning of traffic signs. Discuss how traffic laws keep people safe, and how police officers make sure people follow the laws.*

Transportation

We use many different forms of transportation. Some people operate motor vehicles as an occupation.

SCIENCE EXPERIENCE

- Let the children find pictures of different types of transportation: trucks, taxis, planes, buses, vans, and others. Try to get two pictures of each.
- Have the children cut out pictures of people that operate each form of transportation: truck drivers, taxi drivers, airplane pilots, bus drivers, moms and dads, and others. Try to find two pictures of each.
- Have the children mount the pictures on construction paper. They can match transportation pictures with workers, or match drivers with vehicles.

MATERIALS

magazines
scissors
glue
construction paper

WORDS TO DISCUSS

airplane
airplane pilot
bus
bus driver
car
ship
ship captain
train
train conductor

EXPLANATION

Learning about ways people travel from one place to another can expand a child's understanding of her world.

Roll on Big Wheels

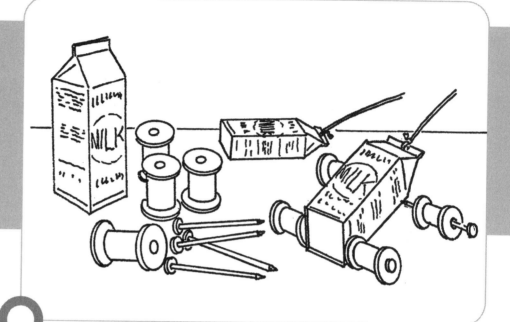

PRINCIPLES

People use machines to make work easier.

MATERIALS

empty milk carton
four spools
two long nails
string

WORDS TO DISCUSS

invent
machine
wheel

SCIENCE EXPERIENCE

○ Tie a string to a milk carton at the spout. Allow the children to pull the milk carton along the top of a table. "How hard is it to pull?"

○ Put the nails through the spools and insert the nails in the sides of the carton. Let the children pull the milk carton. "Is it easier to pull?"

○ "Why did people begin using the wheel?" "If we add things to the milk carton, does it make it easier or harder to pull?"

EXPLANATION

Wheels make jobs easier to perform. It is easier to pull the carton on the spools because the wheel turns smoothly and easily.

90

Creating Colors

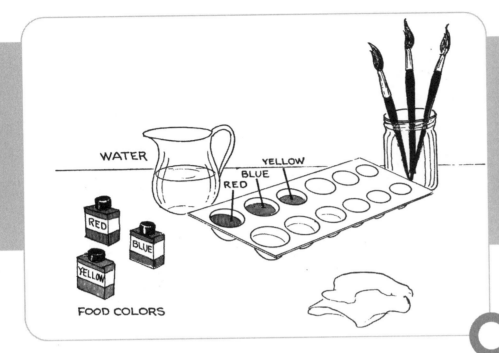

WATER

YELLOW

BLUE

RED

RED

BLUE

YELLOW

FOOD COLORS

PRINCIPLES

The children will learn the names of the primary colors and that combinations of primary colors create new colors.

SCIENCE EXPERIENCE

- ○ Cover a table with newspaper.
- ○ Put out the egg cartons and fill sections half full of water.
- ○ Have the children put primary food colors in three egg sections and encourage them to mix the colors. When mixed, they will create new colors.

MATERIALS

newspaper
white foam egg cartons
  with lids removed
water
red, yellow, and blue
  food coloring

WORDS TO DISCUSS

primary colors (red, blue,
  and yellow)

EXPLANATION

The three primary colors make all other colors, depending on how they are mixed.

91

Collections

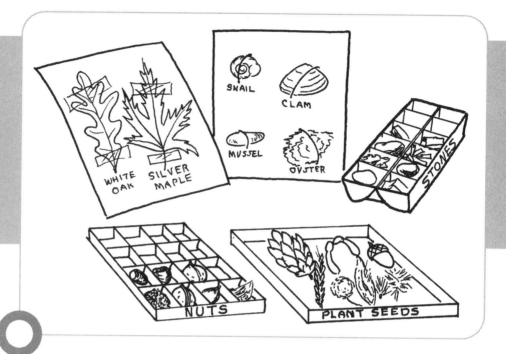

MATERIALS

Natural objects collected from the playground or from the children's yards

WORDS TO DISCUSS

depends on the collection

SCIENCE EXPERIENCE

- Depending on the time of the year and the area in which you live, a variety of things may be collected, such as leaves, wildflowers, shells, seeds, rocks, or nuts.
- Let the children classify their collections by color and by shape.
- Provide picture books, dictionaries, cut-out pictures, seed catalogs, shell books, and other resources for the children to use to identify their collections.

EXPLANATION

Collecting natural objects can help children understand how things can look different although they are essentially the same. For example, leaves can be the same shape but different colors, and rocks can be the same color but different shapes.

92

Food Book

CUT OUT

PAPER SCRAPS

PASTE

MAGAZINES

FOOD BOOK

Different foods taste different. Cooking makes a difference in the taste of foods. Usually our taste determines whether we like a food.

SCIENCE EXPERIENCE

- Let the children go through the magazines and select pictures of foods or dishes they like or dislike.
- Encourage the children to cut out the pictures and glue them in the book.
- Record what the children say about their feelings about the foods they have selected.

MATERIALS

magazines
scissors
glue
marker
materials for making a
    book (see Making a
    Seed Book, page 61)

WORDS TO DISCUSS

vocabulary words
    appropriate to foods
    selected

EXPLANATION

Foods taste good or bad to different people. Children will learn that not everyone tastes foods the same way or likes the same foods all of the time, even though our tongues taste things in the same way.

Miscellaneous Experiments

Airport by Byron Barton

Bear's Playschool Weighing: Weigh It Up by Andy Cooke

Big Movers: With Movable Parts by Matt Mitter

Boats by Anne F. Rockwell

I Love Boats by Flora M. Donnell

A Color of His Own by Leo Lionni

The Colors by Monique Felix

Colors Everywhere by Tana Hoban

Green Bear by Alan Rogers

The Little Airplane by Lois Lenski

Little Blue and Little Yellow by Leo Lionni

The Little Red Lighthouse and the Great Gray Bridge
   by Hildegarde Swift

Maisy Drives the Bus by Lucy Cousins

Milk to Ice Cream (Welcome Books: How Things Are Made)
   by Inez Snyder

Mouse Paint by Ellen Stohl Walsh

Pilot Mom by Kathleen Benner Duble

The Post Office Book: Mail and How It Moves by Gail Gibbons

Sailing to the Sea by Mary Claire Helldorfer

Sarah's Boat by Douglas Alvord

Signs at the Airport by Mary Hill

Signs on the Road by Mary Hill

The Smushy Bus by Leslie Helakoski

This Is the Way We Go to School by Edith Baer

Wheels (Little Surprises) by Michael Evans

Wheels Go Round by Yvonne Hooker

Who Said Red? by Mary Serfozo

Workboats by Jan Adkins

The World Around Us by Rosemary Wells

Teacher Resource Books

Active Experiences for Active Children: Science by Carol Seefeldt and Alice Galper

The All-New Kids' Stuff Book of Creative Science Experiences for the Young Child by Imogene Forte and Joy MacKenzie

Bite-Sized Science: Activities for Children in 15 Minutes or Less by John H. Falk, Kristi S. Rosenberg, and Bonnie Matthews

Discovery Science: Preschool Explorations for the Early Years by David A. Winnett

Easy Answers to First Science Questions About Animals by Querida L. Pierce

Everybody Has a Body by Robert E. Rockwell

Exploring Science in Early Childhood: A Developmental Approach by Karen K. Lind

Fun With My Five Senses: Activities to Build Learning Readiness by Jill Frankel Hauser and Sarah A. Williamson

The Giant Encyclopedia of Science Activities for Children 3 to 6 edited by Kathy Charner

Investigating Science With Young Children by Rosemary Althouse

The Little Hands Nature Book by Nancy Castaldo

More Mudpies to Magnets by Robert A. Williams, Robert E. Rockwell, and Elizabeth Sherwood

More Science Experiments You Can Eat by Vicki Cobb

More Than Magnets: Exploring the Wonders of Science in Preschool and Kindergarten by Sally Moomaw

Mudpies to Magnets by Robert A. Williams, Robert E. Rockwell, and Elizabeth Sherwood

Poems Children Will Sit Still For by Eva Moore, Beatrice Schenck de Regniers, and Mary White

A Practical Guide to Early Childhood Curriculum by Evelyn Petersen

Resources for Creative Teaching in Early Childhood Education by Bonnie Mack Fleming and Darlene Softley Hamilton

Science by Evan-Moor Educational Publishers

Science Experiences for the Early Childhood Years: An Integrated Affective Approach by Jean Durgin Harlan

Science Is Simple by Peggy Ashbrook

Science to Go: Fact and Fiction Learning Packs by Judy Sauerteig

Science, Air, and Space Activities: Folder Games for the Classroom Adapted for Preschool by Jane Hodges-Caballero

Science, Math, and Nutrition for Toddlers: Setting the Stage for Serendipity by Rita Schrank

The Solar System (Preschool Projects) by Beth Seidel

Teaching Science for All Children by Ralph E. Martin

Water All Around by Catherine Nichols

96

Index

A

Adaptation, 30
Adhesive spray, 14
Air
    books about, 22
    experiences, 15–21, 36, 42
    pressure, 17, 19–21, 36, 79
    transfer, 18
    vibrations, 68
Airplanes, 89
Amphibians, 31
Animals
    babies, 24, 31
    books about, 33–34
    caring for, 25, 30–31, 84
    experiences, 23–32
    farm, 8
    homes, 29
    plastic, 32
Ant farms, 12
    homemade, 26
Anthills, 26
Ants, 26
Apples, 10, 56
    seeds, 56, 63
Aquariums, 12, 14, 25, 31, 84
Arrowheads, 36
Attraction, 38, 40, 50
Avocados, 63

B

Baby food jars, 59, 71
Bacon, 71
Bags
    paper, 14, 20
    sandwich, 56
    zippered plastic, 14

Balance scales, 12, 49
Balloons, 14, 18, 20, 39–40
Balls, 14, 42, 45
Bananas, 10
Beans, 63
    dried, 58
    growing, 58–59
    how they grow, 60
Bells, 67
Blindfolds, 71–72
Blocks, 48
Bookcases, 12
Books, 14, 67, 72
    about air, 22
    about animals, 14, 33–34
    about plants, 14, 64
    about the senses, 74
    about the environment, 53
    about water, 85
    food, 93
    paperback, 20
    picture, 24, 92
    seed, 61
    teacher resource, 95
Boots, 46
Bottles, 14, 18
Bowls, 51
Boxes, 62, 68
Breathing, 84
Broccoli, 62
Bubbles, 16, 18
Bulletin boards, 60
Burlap, 73
Burrows, 29–30
Buses, 89
Butcher paper, 37

C

Cages, 14, 25
Cake pans, 14, 51
    disposable, 27
    square, 68
Cans, 14, 20, 83
Cantaloupes, 56
Captivity, 25, 27
Carbon dioxide, 32
Cardboard, 36, 79
Carrots, 10, 30, 57, 62, 70
    puzzles, 10
Cars, 89
    homemade, 90
Catalogs
    clothing, 47
    seed, 8, 56, 61, 63
Chairs, 14, 17
Chalk, 67
Charcoal, 14
Charting, 41
Cheese cubes, 70
Cherries, 56
Chickens, 60
Chocolate milk, 70
Classrooms
    fitting science in, 10
    science center, 12–13
Clay, 73
Clothes trees, 46
Clothes
    doll's, 66
    dress-up, 46
Clothesline, 66
Clouds, 77
Cloves, 71
Collections, 92

BUBBLES, RAINBOWS, & WORMS

Colors, 16, 92
    experience with, 91
Combs, 14, 40
Compasses, 38
Compression, 21
Condensation, 76–77, 83
Conservation, 7
Construction paper, 14, 16, 28,
    37, 44, 51, 61, 89
Containers, 18, 25
Cooking oil, 81
Corks, 14, 38
Cornmeal, 30
Cotton, 14, 26, 59
Crayons, 14, 16
Crystals, 51–52
Cups, 16
    measuring, 51
    paper, 14, 51, 78
    plastic, 21, 51
    Styrofoam, 69

D

Dark rooms, 39
Demonstrations, 8
Density, 80
Dew, 83
Dictionaries, 92
Digging tools, 14, 26
Directions, 36, 38
Dishpans, 62
Dissolving, 81
Ditto sheets, 8
Doll clothes, 66
Dress-up clothes, 46
Drinking glasses, 79
    glass, 14
    plastic, 14, 21

E

Earth, 43, 45
Earthworms, 30
Egg cartons, 14

Styrofoam, 91
Emotional support, 10
Energy, 44
Environment, 25–30
    books about, 53
    experiences with, 35–52
Epsom salt, 14, 51
Erasers, 36
Evaporation, 82
Experiences
    with air, 15–22
    with animals, 23–34
    with collections, 92
    with colors, 91
    with food, 93
    with plants, 55–63
    with the environment,
      35–52
    with the senses, 65-73
    with transportation, 88–90
    with water, 75–84

F

Fabric, 14, 42
    seasonal, 46–47
    textured, 73, 81
    wool, 39–40
Farm animals, 8
Feathers, 14, 36
Ferns, 32
Field trips, 8
Fine motor skills, 10, 14, 19,
    24, 37, 47, 48, 61, 63, 89,
    91, 93
Fish, 12, 84
Fish food, 84
Fish tanks, 84
Fishing weights, 14
Flashlights, 14, 43
Flour, 8
Flow, 81
Flowerpots, 58
Food coloring, 14, 91

Foods, 70, 93
Freezing, 41, 78
Friction, 40
Frogs, 8, 31, 60
    eggs, 31
Frost, 83
Fruits, 10, 56
    pictures of, 56
    salad, 56
    seeds, 56, 63
Funnels, 81
Furniture, 12

G

Garden soil, 58, 62
Gardening activities
    beans, 58–59
    crystals, 51–52
    indoor, 62
    terrariums, 32
    without seeds, 57
Germination, 59
Glass jars, 81, 82
    baby food, 59, 71
    large, 30–32, 77
    one-gallon, 26, 30–32
    six-liter, 32
    three-liter, 31–32
    two-gallon, 30, 32
Globes, 14, 45
Glue, 14, 24, 29, 37, 47, 61, 63,
    89, 93
Grapefruit juice, 70
Gravel, 14, 30, 32
Gravity, 48–49
Grouping, 46–47
Growing, 24, 31, 56, 58–61

H

Habitats, 26–27, 29–30
Hatching, 31
Hats, 46
Health, 46

Heat, 44
Heredity, 24, 31
Hole punches, 29
Hot plates, 14, 76
Humidity, 82

I
Ice, 78
    crushed, 83
    cubes, 73, 77
Insects, 25–27

J
Jars. See Glass jars
Jungles, 29

K
Kale seeds, 62

L
Lamps, 14
Language development, 13,
    62–63, 91
    science and, 10
Lemon extract, 71
Lemons, 56
Lettuce, 30
    seeds, 62
Lids, 32
    glass, 76, 77
    screw-on, 67
Light, 16, 37, 43–44
Lightning, 39
Lima beans, 59, 63
Liquid detergent, 14, 16, 66
Liquids/solids, 51
Lunch bags, 20

M
Magazines, 24, 29, 47, 50, 56,
    61, 89, 93
Magnetizing, 38
Magnets, 14, 38, 40, 50
Magnifiers, 12

Magnifying glasses, 12, 14
Manila paper, 61
Marbles, 8, 81
Markers, 14, 56, 61, 82, 93
Masking tape, 37, 43, 59
Matching, 24, 56, 61, 63, 89
Materials, 8–9
    list, 14
    real objects, 9
Mayonnaise jars, 77
Measuring cups, 51
Measuring spoons, 51
Measuring
    devices, 12
    temperature, 41, 44
    weight, 49
Meat trays, 14, 50
Melting, 78
Metal, 50, 73
    dishpans, 62
    nuts, 51
    tubs, 12
Microscopes, 14, 51
Milk, 8
    cartons, 8, 14, 90
    chocolate, 70
    whole, 70
Miniature animals, 32
Mirrors, 12
    full-length, 46
    hand, 46
Mittens, 46
Modeling, 10
Moisture, 77
Moss, 32
Music, 68
Musical instruments, 68
Mustard, 71
Mustard green seeds, 62

N
Nails, 8, 14, 81, 90
Natural objects, 92

Needles, 14, 38
Nests, 29
Newspaper, 91
Night and day, 43

O
Onions, 71
Opposites, 43, 46, 67, 70
Oranges, 10, 56
    seeds, 56
Outdoor activities, 16, 26,
    28, 36, 41–42, 44, 51, 62,
    66, 88
Oxygen, 32

P
Pans, 21, 38, 51, 76
    cake, 14, 27, 51, 68
    pie, 51
    shallow, 80, 82
Paper, 14, 17, 40, 67, 73
    butcher, 37
    construction, 14, 16, 28,
    37, 44, 51, 61, 89
    dark, 26, 37, 44, 51
    heavy, 24
    manila, 61
    newspaper, 91
Paper bags, 14, 18, 20
Paper cups, 14, 51, 78
Paper towels, 14, 21, 71
Parachutes, 42
Parsnips, 10
Peaches, 10, 56
    seeds, 56, 63
Peas, 62
Pencils, 14, 36, 48, 51
Pens, 67
Pets, 25
Pickle jars, 77
Pickles, 70
Pictures
    animal babies, 24

animal development, 60

animal homes, 29

animals, 29

floating and sinking objects, 80

foods, 93

fruit, 56

nature items, 92

seed development, 60

transportation, 89

Pie pans, 51

Pins, 14

straight, 36

Plants, 8, 10, 14, 31–32

books about, 64

experiences with, 55–63

seedless, 57

Plaster of Paris, 14, 27

Plastic

bags, 14, 56

bottles, 14, 18

cups, 51

dishpans, 62

drinking glasses, 14, 21

trays, 80

tubing, 14

tubs, 12

zippered bags, 14

Police badges, 88

Pond water, 31

Popcorn, 62

Poster board, 24, 29, 41, 47, 63

Potting soil, 14, 30, 32, 58, 62

Powdered detergent, 14

Predators, 29

Primary colors, 91

Prisms, 14

Produce trays, 14, 50

Puzzles

animal baby, 24

homemade, 10

Q

Questions

children's, 8

open-ended, 11

R

Racks, 46

Radishes, 70

seeds, 62

Rags, 88

Rainbows, 16

Raincoats, 46

Raisins, 70

Replacement, 21

Representation, 43, 45, 47

Reproduction, 27, 56

Rock salt, 14, 83

Rocks, 8, 14, 81

Roots, 57

Ropes, 12, 88

Rotation, 43, 45

Rubber bands, 14, 20, 68

Rubber gloves, 14

Rubber tubing, 14

Rubbing alcohol, 78

Rugs, 12

S

Safety notes

boiling water, 76–77

sunburns, 44

Salt, 8, 14, 78, 81

Sand, 14, 32, 58, 62

Sandals, 46

Sandpaper, 73

Scales, 14

balance, 12, 59

spring, 12

Scarves, 46

Science center, 12–13

locating, 12

materials, 12, 14

Screen wire, 14, 27

Screens, 25

Sea glass, 8

Seasons, 46–47, 78

Sediment, 82

Seeds, 10, 56, 62

beans, 58–59

books, 61

catalogs, 8, 56, 61, 63, 92

fruit, 56, 63

vegetable, 62

Senses, 10

books about, 74

experiences with, 65–73

smell, 71–72

sound, 67–69

taste, 70

touch, 66, 73

Sequencing

activities, 60

orderly, 9

Shadows, 37, 45

Shapes, 10, 16, 63, 92

Shelves, 12

Ships, 89

Shirts, 46

Silhouettes, 37

Silk, 73

Sink plungers, 14, 19

Smell, 71–72

Snack time, 56, 62, 70

Snake skins, 8

Solutions, 51

Sorting, 49–50, 56, 92

Sound, 67–69

Sparks, 39–40

Spider webs, 28

Spiders, 27–28

Sponges, 14, 27

Spools, 90

Spray adhesive, 14, 28

Spring scales, 12

Springs, 14

Staplers, 61
Static electricity, 39–40
Steam, 76–77
Sticks, 14, 27, 36, 45, 88
Stools, 12
Straws, 14, 16, 18, 20, 36
String, 14, 42, 51, 69, 90
Styrofoam
    cups, 69
    egg cartons, 91
Suction, 19, 79
Sugar, 51, 81
Sun, 43–45, 51, 58–59
Sweaters, 46
Sweet potatoes, 57

T
Tables, 12
Tacks, 8
Tadpoles, 31
Tagboard, 88
Talcum powder, 14, 28
Taste, 70
Teaching
    modeling, 10
    ten commandments of, 11
Teamwork, 26
Tempera paint, 14
Temperature, 41, 44
    and water, 76–78
Terrariums
    homemade, 32
Textures, 73
Thermometers, 14, 41, 44
Thumbtacks, 14, 37
Tissues, 81
Toothpicks, 57, 69
Touch, 66, 73
Toys, 48
Traffic signs, 88
Trains, 89

Transportation
    experiences with, 88–90
Tricycles, 88
Tubers, 57
Tubes, 81
Tubs
    large, 12
    metal, 12
    plastic, 12
Turnips, 10

U
Ultraviolet radiation, 44

V
Vacuums, 19, 79
Vanilla extract, 71
Vegetables
    leafy, 14, 31
    seeds, 62
Vests, 46
Vibration, 68–69
Vines, 57
Vocabulary, 13

W
Wagons, 88
Washers, 51
Water, 16, 18, 21, 32, 38, 51,
    57–59, 66, 91
    books about, 85
    experiences with, 75–84
    pond, 31
Water tank, 31
Watermelon seeds, 63
Weather
    clouds, 77
    dressing for, 46
    evaporation, 82
    frost, 83
    lightning, 39
    seasons, 46–47

    temperature, 41
    wind, 36
Weight, 49, 51
    of air, 18–19
    water and, 80
Wet and dry, 21, 66
Wheels, 14, 90
Whistles, 88
Wind, 36
Winter coats, 46
Wire cylinder, 27
Wood
    blocks, 45
    boxes, 62
Wool, 39–40

Y
Yarn, 14, 29

Z
Zippers, 67

102

Book Index

1, 2, 3 to the Zoo by Eric Carle, 33

A

A, B, Cedar: An Alphabet of Trees by George Ella Lyon, 53

Active Experiences for Active Children: Science by Carol Seefeldt & Alice Galper, 95

Air Is All Around You by Franklyn M. Branley, 22

Air—Our Environment by McDougall, Littell, & Co., 22

Airplanes and Flying Machines by Pascale de Bourgoing, 22

Airport by Byron Barton, 94

The All-New Kids' Stuff Book of Creative Science Experiences for the Young Child by Imogene Forte & Joy MacKenzie, 95

The Amazing Air Balloon by Jean Van Leeuwen, 22

Animal Babies by Holly Ann Shelowitz, 33

Animal Colors by Brian Wildsmith, 33

Animals in Winter by Henrietta Bancroft, 33

Any Room for Me? by Loek Koopmans, 53

B

Bear's Playschool Weighing: Weigh It Up by Andy Cooke, 94

Bedtime for Francis by Russell Hoban, 53

Beetles and Bugs by Audrey Wood, 33

The Berenstain Bears Don't Pollute by Jan & Stan Berenstain, 53

Big Movers With Movable Parts by Matt Mitter, 94

Birds by Brian Wildsmith, 33

Bite-Sized Science: Activities for Children in 15 Minutes or Less by John H. Falk et al., 95

Boats by Anne F. Rockwell, 94

Bubble, Bubble by Mercer Mayer, 22

Bubbly Bubble by Colleen A. Hitchcock, 22

C

Can You See the Wind? by Allan Fowler, 22

Chrysanthemum by Kevin Henkes, 64

Cloud Book by Julian May, 85

The Cloud Book by Tomie dePaola, 85

A Color of His Own by Leo Lionni, 94

Colors Everywhere by Tana Hoban, 94

The Colors by Monique Felix, 94

Connections: Finding Out About the Environment by David Suzuki, 53

Crictor by Tomi Ungerer, 33

Crinkleroot's Guide to Knowing the Trees by Jim Aronsky, 64

Curious George and the Hot Air Balloon by H.A. Rey, 22

D

Discovery Science: Preschool Explorations for the Early Years by David A. Winnett, 95

A Drop Around the World by Barbara Shaw McKinney, 85

E

Early Morning in the Barn by Nancy Tafuri, 33, 74

Earthworms by Chris Henwood, 33

Easy Answers to First Science Questions About Animals by Querida L. Pierce, 95

Eating the Alphabet: Fruits and Vegetables from A to Z by Lois Ehlert, 64

The Empty Pot by Demi, 64

Everybody Has a Body by Robert E. Rockwell et al., 95

Everybody Needs a Rock by Byrd Baylor, 53

Exploring Science in Early Childhood: A Developmental Approach by Karen K. Lind, 95

An Extraordinary Egg by Leo Lionni, 33

F

Feel the Wind by Arthur Dorros, 22

Feeling Things by Allan Fowler, 74

Felix and the 400 Frogs by Jon Buller & Susan Schade, 33

First Comes Spring by Anne F. Rockwell, 64

The Five Senses by Beth Sidel, 74

The Five Senses by Keith Faulkner, 74

Flash, Crash, Rumble, and Roll by Franklyn M. Branley, 53

Flower Garden by Even Bunting, 64

Flowers by Ivan Anatta, 64

Follow the Water From Brook to Ocean by Arthur Dorros, 85

The *Frederick* books by Leo Lionni, 33

Fresh Fall Leaves by Betsy Franco, 64

Frog and Toad Together by Arnold Lobel, 53

Frog on His Own by Mercer Mayer, 33

Frogs and Toads and Tadpoles, Too by Allan Fowler, 33

From Seed to Plant by Gail Gibbons, 64

From Seed to Sunflower by Gerald Legg, 64

From Tadpole to Frog by Wendy Pfeffer, 33

Fun With My Five Senses: Activities to Build Learning Readiness by Jill Frankel Hauser & Sarah A. Williamson, 95

Fuzzy Yellow Ducklings by Matthew Van Fleet, 74

G

The Giant Encyclopedia of Science Activities for Children 3 to 6 edited by Kathy Charner, 95

Gilberto and the Wind by Marie Hall Ets, 22

The Giving Tree by Shel Silverstein, 64

The Great Balloon Race by Rosie Heywood, 22

Green Bear by Alan Rogers, 94

Growing Frogs by Vivian French, 33

Growing Vegetable Soup by Lois Ehlert, 64

H

Have You Seen Trees? by Joanne Oppenheim, 64

Hearing (The Library of the Five Senses and the Sixth Sense) by Sue Hurwitz, 74

Hearing by Maria Rius, 74

Hearing Sounds by Sally Hewitt, 74

Hearing Things by Allan Fowler, 74

Hot-Air Henry by Mary Calhoun, 22

A House Is a House for Me by Mary Ann Hoberman, 53

How Do Apples Grow? by Betsy Maestro, 64

How Do You Know It's Fall? by Allan Fowler, 53

How Do You Know It's Summer? by Allan Fowler, 53

Hungry Animals: My First Look at the Food Chain by Pamela Hickman, 33

I Am Water by Jean Marzollo, 85

I Can Tell by Touching by Carolyn Otto, 53

I Like Weather by Aileen Fisher, 22

I Love Boats by Flora M. Donnell, 94

I Wonder Why Soap Makes Bubbles: And Other Questions About Science by Barbara Taylor, 22

Intuition (The Library of the Five Senses and the Sixth Sense) by Sue Hurwitz, 74

Investigating Science With Young Children by Rosemary Althouse, 95

Is This a House for Hermit Crab? by Megan McDonald, 53

It Could Still Be a Flower by Allan Fowler, 64

It Could Still Be a Lake by Allan Fowler, 85

It Could Still Be a Tree by Allan Fowler, 64

It Could Still Be Water by Allan Fowler, 85

It's Raining, It's Pouring by Kin Eagle, 85

J

Jack's Garden by Henry Cole, 64

Jump, Frog, Jump! by Robert Kalan, 33

L

Let's Go Home, Little Bear by Martin Waddell & Barbara Firth, 33

Let's Try It Out in the Air: Hands-On Early-Learning Science Activities by Seymour Simon, 22

The Life and Times of the Ant by Charles Micucci, 33

Listen to the Rain by Bill Martin, Jr., & John Archambault, 74

The Listening Walk by Paul Showers, 74

The Little Airplane by Lois Lenski, 94

Little Blue and Little Yellow by Leo Lionni, 94

Little Cloud by Eric Carle, 85

The Little Hands Nature Book by Nancy Castaldo, 95

Little Polar Bear by Hans de Beer, 33

The Little Red Lighthouse and the Great Gray Bridge by Hildegarde Swift, 94

Look What I Did With a Leaf! by Morteza E. Sohi, 64

M

The Magic School Bus on the Ocean Floor by Joanna Cole, 33

The Magic School Bus Wet All Over: A Book About the Weather Cycle by Patricia Reif, 85

The Magic School Bus: At the Water Works by Joanna Cole, 85

Maisy Drives the Bus by Lucy Cousins, 94

Mama Don't Allow by Thacher Hurd, 74

Milk to Ice Cream (Welcome Books: How Things Are Made) by Inez Snyder, 94

Millicent and the Wind by Robert Munsch, 22

Miss Spider's Tea Party by David Kirk, 33

More Mudpies to Magnets by Robert A. Williams et al., 95

More Science Experiments You Can Eat by Vicki Cobb, 95

More Than Magnets: Exploring the Wonders of Science in Preschool and Kindergarten by Sally Moomaw, 95

Mouse Paint by Ellen Stohl Walsh, 94

Mudpies to Magnets by Robert A. Williams et al., 95

My Five Senses by Aliki, 74

My Visit to the Dinosaurs by Aliki, 53

N

A New Butterfly: My First Look at Metamorphosis by Pamela Hickman, 33

Night Sounds, Morning Colors by Rosemary Wells, 74

Noises: Let's Learn by Anna Nilsen, 74

O

The Ocean Alphabet Book by Jerry Palotta, 33

One Bean by Anne F. Rockwell, 64

One Hundred Hungry Ants by Elinor J. Pinczes, 33

Owl at Home by Arnold Lobel, 33

Owl Babies by Martin Waddell, 34

Owl Moon by Jane Yolen, 34

P

Papa, Please Get the Moon for Me by Eric Carle, 53

Pick, Pull, Snap! Where Once a Flower Bloomed by Lola M. Schaefer, 64

Pilot Mom by Kathleen Benner Duble, 94

The Planets in Our Solar System by Franklyn M. Branley, 53

The Planets by Gail Gibbons, 53

Planting a Rainbow by Lois Ehlert, 64

Plants That Never Ever Bloom by Ruth Heller, 64

Plants! by Andrew Haslam, 64

Poems Children Will Sit Still For by Eva Moore et al., 95

Pop! A Book About Bubbles by Kimberly Brubaker Bradley, 22

The Post Office Book: Mail and How It Moves by Gail Gibbons, 94

Pots and Pans by Patricia Hubbell, 74

A Practical Guide to Early Childhood Curriculum by Evelyn Petersen, 95

Python's Party by Brian Wildsmith, 34

R

Rain by Peter Spier, 85

Rain by Robert Kalan, 85

Rain Drop Splash by Alvin Tresselt, 85

The Reason for a Flower by Ruth Heller, 64

Recycle Every Day by Nancy Elizabeth Wallace, 53

Recycle! A Handbook for Kids by Gail Gibbons, 53

Red Leaf, Yellow Leaf by Lois Ehlert, 64

Resources for Creative Teaching in Early Childhood Education by Bonnie Mack et al., 95

The River by Mark Pollard, 85

Rooster's Off to See the World by Eric Carle, 34

Round and Square by Miriam Schlein, 74

S

Sadie and the Snowman by Allen Morgan, 85

Sailing to the Sea by Mary Claire Helldorfer, 94

Sarah's Boat by Douglas Alvord, 94

The Science Book of Air by Neil Ardley & Nicole Fauteux, 22

Science by Evan-Moor Educational Publishers, 95

Science Experiences for the Early Childhood Years: An Integrated Affective Approach by Jean Durgin Harlan, 95

Science in the Air (How and Why Science) by World Book, 22

Science Is Simple by Peggy Ashbrook, 95

Science Play! by Jill Frankel Hauser, 53

Science to Go: Fact and Fiction Learning Packs by Judy Sauerteig, 95

Science With Air by Usborne Books, 22

Science, Air, and Space Activities: Folder Games for the Classroom Adapted for Preschool by Jane Hodges-Caballero, 95

Science, Math, and Nutrition for Toddlers: Setting the Stage for Serendipity by Rita Schrank, 95

The Seasons of Arnold's Apple Tree by Gail Gibbons, 64

See, Hear, Touch, Taste, and Smell by Melvin Berger, 74

A Seed Grows: My First Look at a Plant's Life Cycle by Pamela Hickman, 64

Sense It, Hear It by Maile & Wren, 74

Sense It, See It by Maile & Wren, 74

Sense It, Smell It by Maile & Wren, 74

Sense It, Taste It by Maile & Wren, 74

Sense It, Touch It by Maile & Wren, 74

Sense Suspense: A Guessing Game for the Five Senses by Bruce McMillan, 53

Sight (The Library of the Five Senses and the Sixth Sense) by Sue Hurwitz, 74

Signs at the Airport by Mary Hill, 94

Signs on the Road by Mary Hill, 94

Smelling Things by Allan Fowler, 74

The Smushy Bus by Leslie Helakoski, 94

Snow and Ice by Stephen Krensky, 85

Snow Is Falling by Franklyn M. Branley, 85

The Snowy Day by Ezra Jack Keats, 85

The Solar System (Preschool Projects) by Beth Seidel, 95

Sounds All Around by Wendy Pfeffer, 74

SPLASH! by Ann Jonas, 34

Starfish by Edith Thacher Hurd, 34

Stone Soup by Ann McGovern, 53

Storms by Seymour Simon, 53

The Story of Light by Susan L. Roth, 53

The Sun (Planet Library) by Robin Kerrod, 53

The Sun Is Always Shining Somewhere by Allan Fowler, 53

Sun Up, Sun Down by Gail Gibbons, 53

The Sun's Family of Planets by Allan Fowler, 53

T

Taste (The Library of the Five Senses and the Sixth Sense) by Sue Hurwitz, 74

Taste by Maria Rius, 74

Teaching Science for All Children by Ralph E. Martin, 95

Thanks to Cows by Allan Fowler, 34

There's an Alligator Under My Bed by Mercer Mayer, 34

This Is the Way We Go to School by Edith Baer, 94

This Year's Garden by Cynthia Rylant, 64

The Tiny Seed by Eric Carle, 64

Touch (The Library of the Five Senses and the Sixth Sense) by Sue Hurwitz, 74

Touch by Maria Rius, 74

A Tree Is Nice by Janice May Udry, 64

Trees of North America by Christian Frank Brockman, 64

V

Vegetables, Vegetables by Fay Robinson & Allan Fowler, 64

The Very Hungry Caterpillar by Eric Carle, 34

W

Water All Around by Catherine Nichols, 95

Water as a Gas by Helen Frost, 85

Water as a Solid by Helen Frost, 85

The Water Cycle by Helen Frost, 85

Water, Water Everywhere by Mark J. Ranzon, 85

We Need Water by Helen Frost, 85

Weather Words and What They Mean by Gail Gibbons, 22

What Do You Do With a Tail Like This? by Steve Jenkins, 34

What Do You See in a Cloud? by Allan Fowler, 85

What Is a Magnet? by Jim Pipe, 53

What Lives in a Shell? by Kathleen Weidner Zoehfeld, 34

What Magnets Can Do by Allan Fowler, 53

What Makes a Magnet? by Franklyn M. Branley, 53

What Makes a Shadow? by Clyde Robert Bulla, 53

What Makes Day and Night? by Franklyn M. Branley, 53

What Noise? by Debbie MacKinnon, 74

What's Alive? by Kathleen Weidner Zoehfeld, 34

What's Out There? A Book About Space by Lynn Wilson, 53

What's This? by Caroline Mockford, 64

The Wheat We Eat by Allan Fowler, 64

Wheels (Little Surprises) by Michael Evans, 94

Wheels Go Round by Yvonne Hooker, 94

When the Wind Stops by Charlotte Zolotow, 22

Where Do Puddles Go? by Fay Robinson, 85

Where Once There Was a Wood by Denise Fleming, 53

White Snow, Bright Snow by Alvin Tresselt, 85

Who Lives Here? by Dorothea Deprisco, 34

Who Said Red? by Mary Serfozo, 94

Who's Making That Smell? by Jenny Tyler, 74

Why Do Leaves Change Color? by Betsy Maestro, 64

Wiggly Worms by Ladybird Books, 34

Wild Moms! by Ginjer L. Clarke, 34

The Wind Blew by Pat Hutchins, 22, 34

Windy Day by Janet Palazzo, 34

Workboats by Jan Adkins, 94

The World Around Us by Rosemary Wells, 94

Y

You Can't Smell a Flower With Your Ear! by Joanna Cole, 74

You Can't Taste a Pickle With Your Ear by Harriet Ziefert, 74

Z

Zin! Zin! Zin! A Violin by Lloyd Moss, 74

The GIANT Encyclopedia of Theme Activities for Children 2 to 5

Over 600 Favorite Activities Created by Teachers for Teachers
Edited by Kathy Charner

This popular potpourri of over 600 classroom-tested activities actively engages children's imaginations and provides many months of learning fun. Organized into 48 popular themes, from dinosaurs to the circus to outer space, these favorites are the result of a nationwide competition. 511 pages. 1993.

ISBN 0-87659-166-7
Gryphon House / 19216

The GIANT Encyclopedia of Art & Craft Activities for Children 3 to 6

More Than 500 Art & Craft Activities Written by Teachers for Teachers
Edited by Kathy Charner

A comprehensive collection of the best art and craft activities for young children. Teacher-created, classroom-tested art activities to actively engage children's imaginations! The result of a nationwide competition, these art and craft activities are the best of the best. Just the thing to add pizzazz to your day! 568 pages. 2000.

ISBN 0-87659-209-4
Gryphon House / 16854

The GIANT Encyclopedia of Circle Time and Group Activities for Children 3 to 6

Over 600 Favorite Circle Time Activities Created by Teachers for Teachers
Edited by Kathy Charner

Open to any page in this book and you will find an activity written by an experienced teacher for circle or group time. Filled with over 600 activities covering 48 themes, this book is jam-packed with ideas that were tested by teachers in the classroom. 510 pages. 1996.

ISBN 0-87659-181-0
Gryphon House / 16413

The GIANT Encyclopedia of Science Activities for Children 3 to 6

More Than 600 Science Activities Written by Teachers for Teachers
Edited by Kathy Charner

Leave your fears of science behind as our *GIANT Encyclopedia* authors have done. Respond to children's natural curiosity with over 600 teacher-created, classroom-tested activities guaranteed to teach your children about science while they are having fun. 575 pages. 1998.

ISBN 0-87659-193-4
Gryphon House / 18325

Mudpies to Magnets

A Preschool Science Curriculum
*Robert A. Williams, Robert E. Rockwell,
and Elizabeth A. Sherwood*

224 hands-on science experiments and
ideas with step-by-step instructions to
delight and amaze children as they
experience nature, the human body,
electricity, floating and sinking, and
more. 157 pages. 1987.

**ISBN 0-87659-112-8 / Gryphon House
10005**

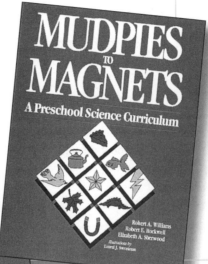

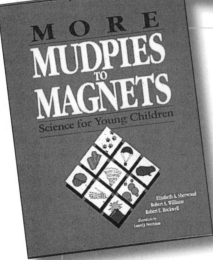

More Mudpies to Magnets

Science for Young Children
*Elizabeth A. Sherwood, Robert A. Williams,
and Robert E. Rockwell*

Develop the natural scientist in every child
with 260 hands-on science activities and
ideas. Build science skills such as
classification, measurement, time and space
concepts, prediction, inference, and
numbers. 205 pages. 1990.

ISBN 0-87659-150-0 / Gryphon House / 10015

Available
at your favorite bookstore,
school supply store, or order
from Gryphon House at
800.638.0928 or
www.gryphonhouse.com.

109

Literacy Play

Dramatic Play Activities That Teach Pre-Reading Skills
Sherrie West and Amy Cox

Children love to pretend, and dramatic play is the perfect environment for practicing and applying literacy concepts. Whether they decide to be firefighters, to open a pet store, or to have a tea party, children will increase their vocabulary, communicate with their friends, and learn to recognize environmental print—all important skills for pre-readers. *Literacy Play* is chock-full of creative dramatic play activities that teach important pre-reading skills while bringing children's imaginations to life! 256 pages. 2004.

ISBN 0-87659-292-2 / Gryphon House 17548

Do You Know the Muffin Man?

Literacy Activities Using Favorite
Rhymes and Songs
Pam Schiller and Thomas Moore

Teach literacy with over 250 familiar songs, rhymes, and activities!

Rhyme, rhythm, and music are an essential part of a quality early childhood program. The authors of the perennial favorite, *Where is Thumbkin?* have created activities children will love to accompany the 250 rhymes and songs in this invaluable new literacy book. Children learn letter recognition, vocabulary, phonemic awareness while they are singing and rhyming. Each rhyme or song includes theme connections so teachers can easily add literacy and music into their daily plans. 256 pages. 2004.

ISBN 0-87659-288-4 / Gryphon House / 19624

Available at your favorite bookstore, school supply store, or order from Gryphon House at 800.638.0928 or www.gryphonhouse.com.

The GIANT Encyclopedia of Kindergarten Activities

Edited by Kathy Charner, Maureen Murphy, and Jennifer Ford

From Autumn Leaf Ornaments to The Recycling Game, kindergarten children will delight in these 600 activities written just for them! In a nationwide contest, teachers submitted their favorite activities and the best of the best are included in this giant resource. This compilation has everything from language and science activities to art, music and movement, and learning centers. You'll find everything you need to keep your kindergarten classes engaged and learning for years to come. 640 pages. 2004.

ISBN 0-87659-285-X / Gryphon House / 18595

The GIANT Encyclopedia of Preschool Activities for Four-Year-Olds

Edited by Kathy Charner and Maureen Murphy

Written just for four-year-olds, this collection of over 600 teacher-created, classroom-tested activities has everything from songs and books to activities in art, circle time, transitions, science, math, language, music and movement, and more! Helpful classroom management techniques are included. This complete resource of the best selections from a national contest is sure to become a classroom favorite. Formerly titled, *It's Great to Be Four*. 624 pages. 2004.

ISBN 0-87659-238-8 / Gryphon House / 14964

The GIANT Encyclopedia of Preschool Activities for Three-Year-Olds

Edited by Kathy Charner and Maureen Murphy

Looking for tried-and-true ways to capture the attention of your three-year-olds? This comprehensive collection of over 600 teacher-created activities provides hours of fun and interesting activities perfectly tailored for this age group. Discover new ways to use everyday items to create fresh, exciting art projects; learn new classroom management techniques from experienced teachers; and find helpful tips for working with three-year-olds. Formerly titled, *It's Great to Be Three*. 576 pages. 2004.

ISBN 0-87659-237-X / Gryphon House / 13963

112